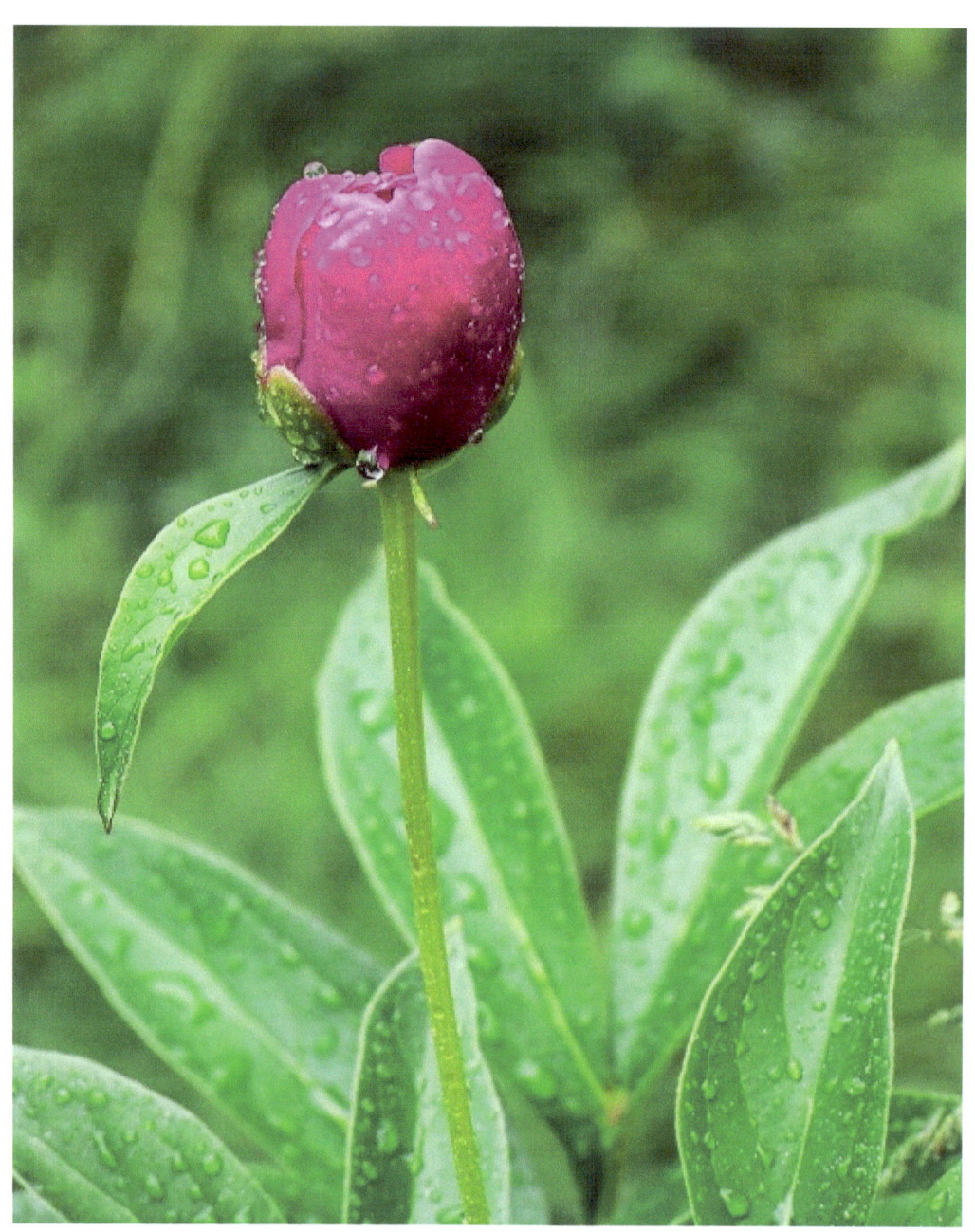

my flowers

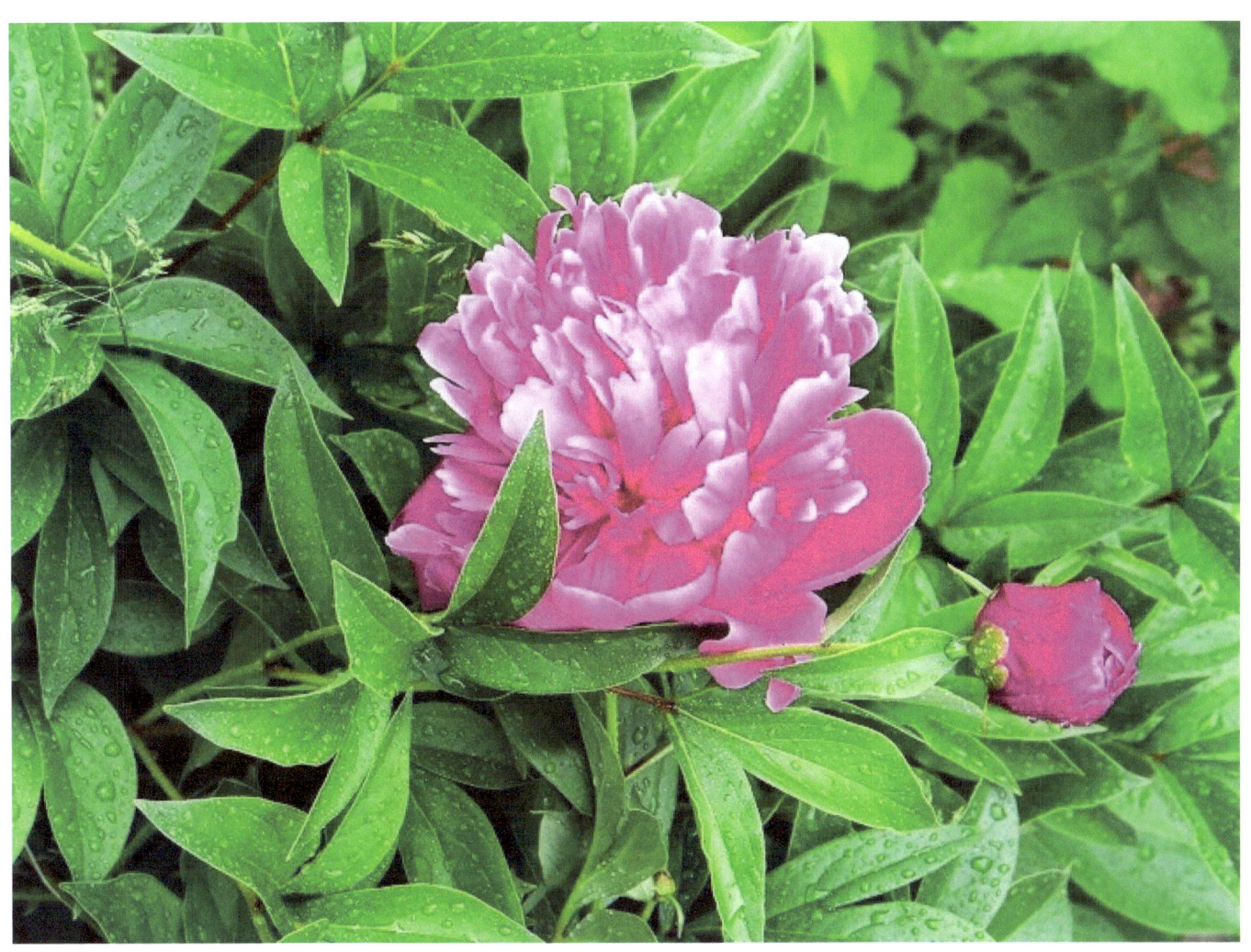

Flowers in my garden

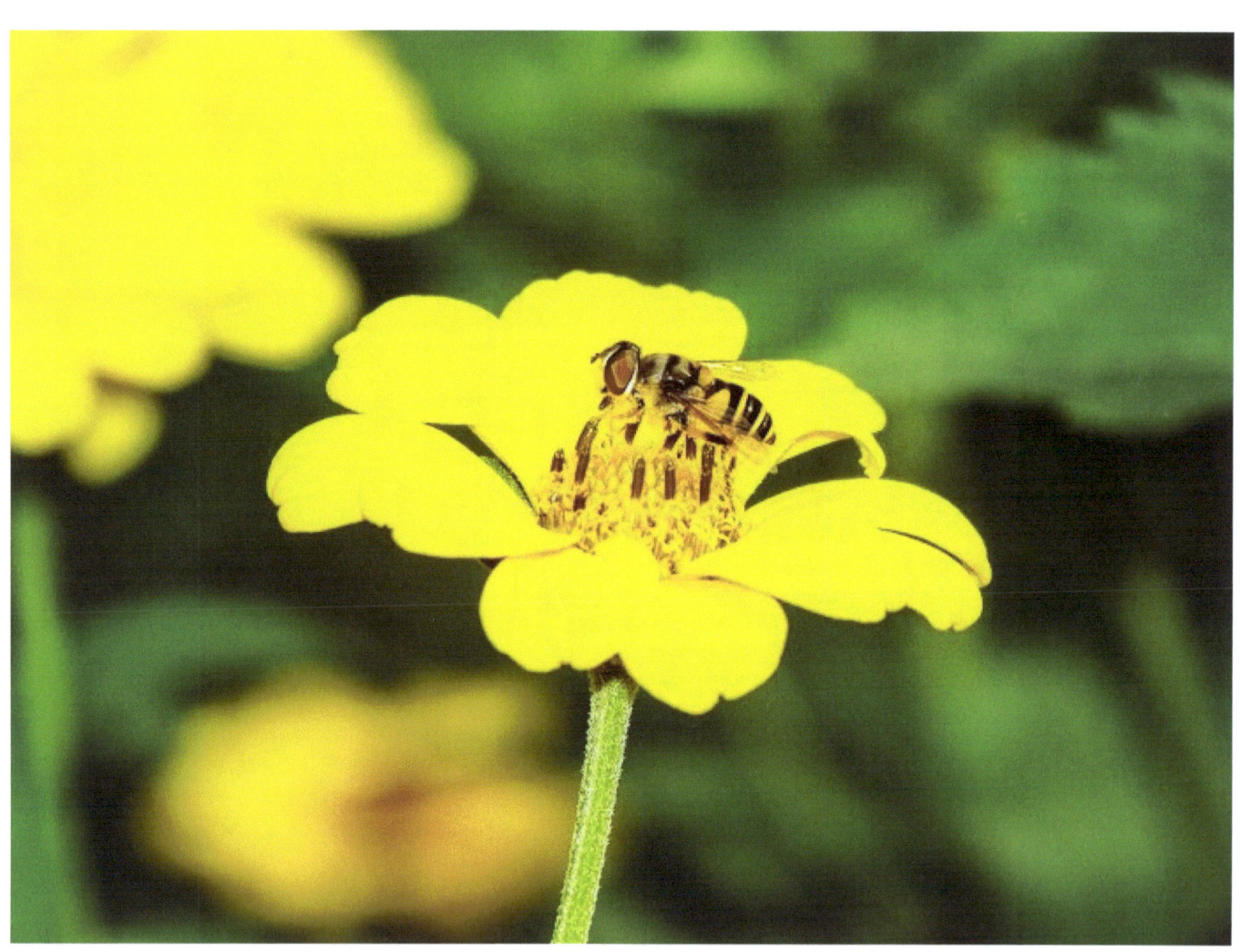

Busy bee in my garden

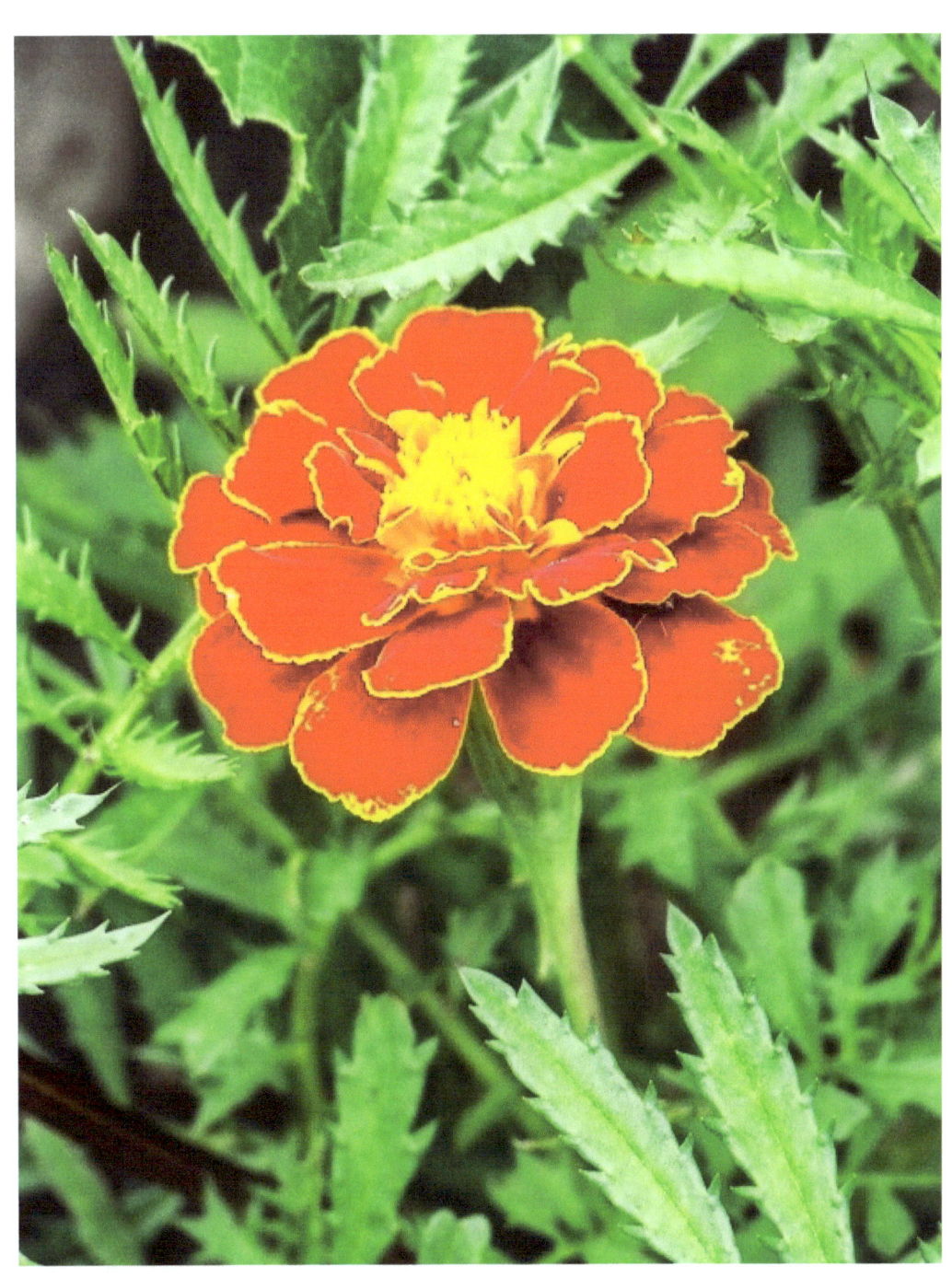

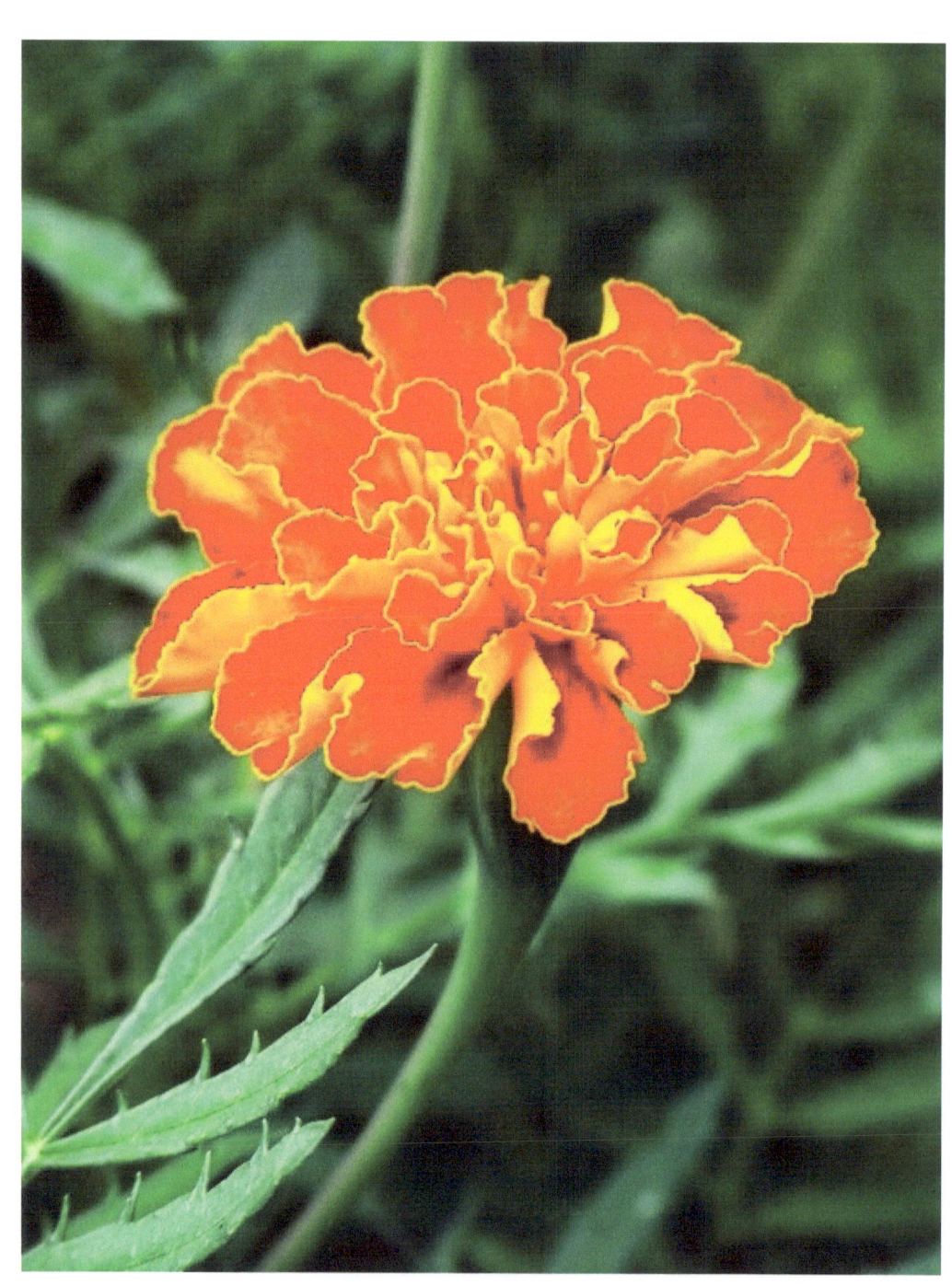

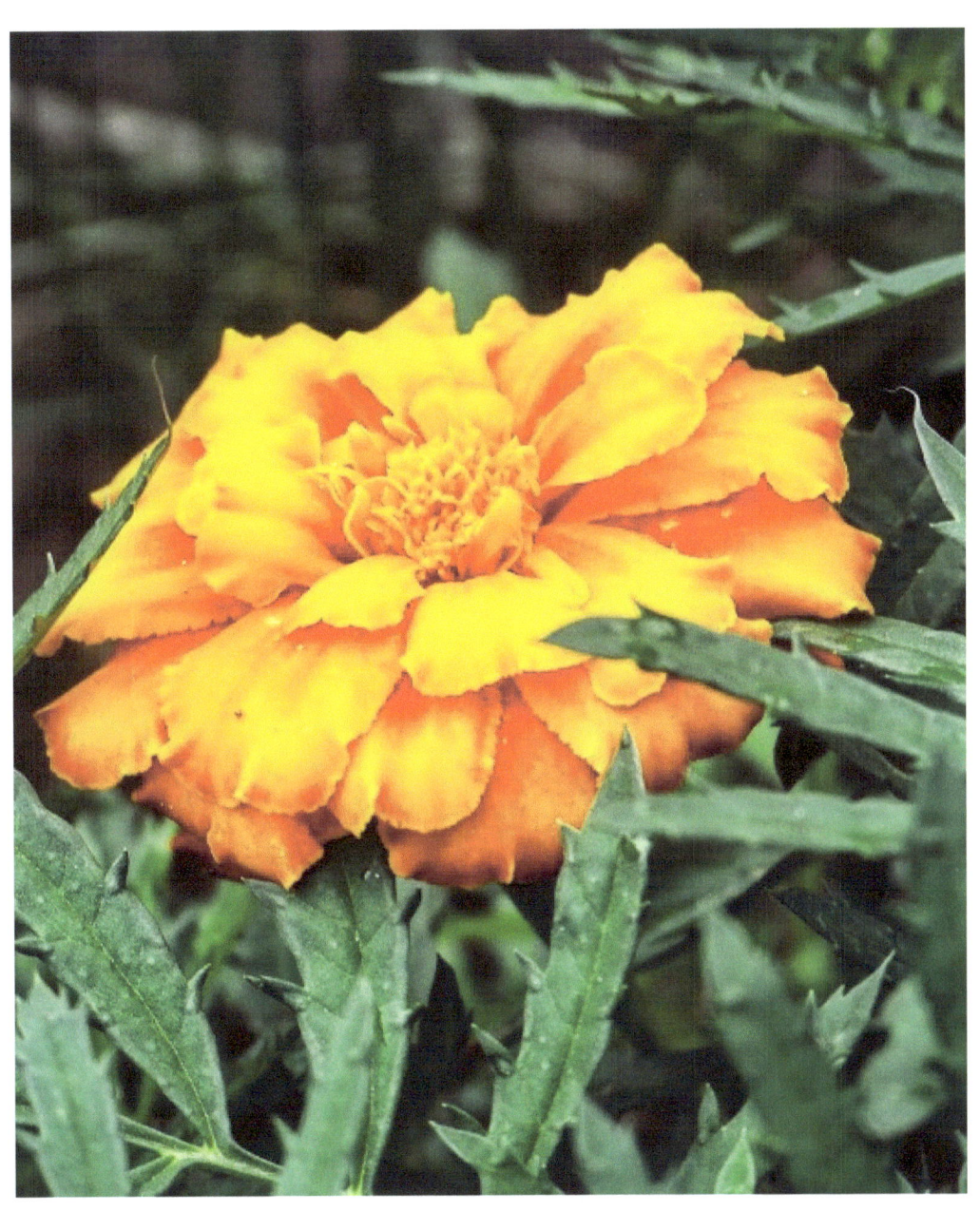

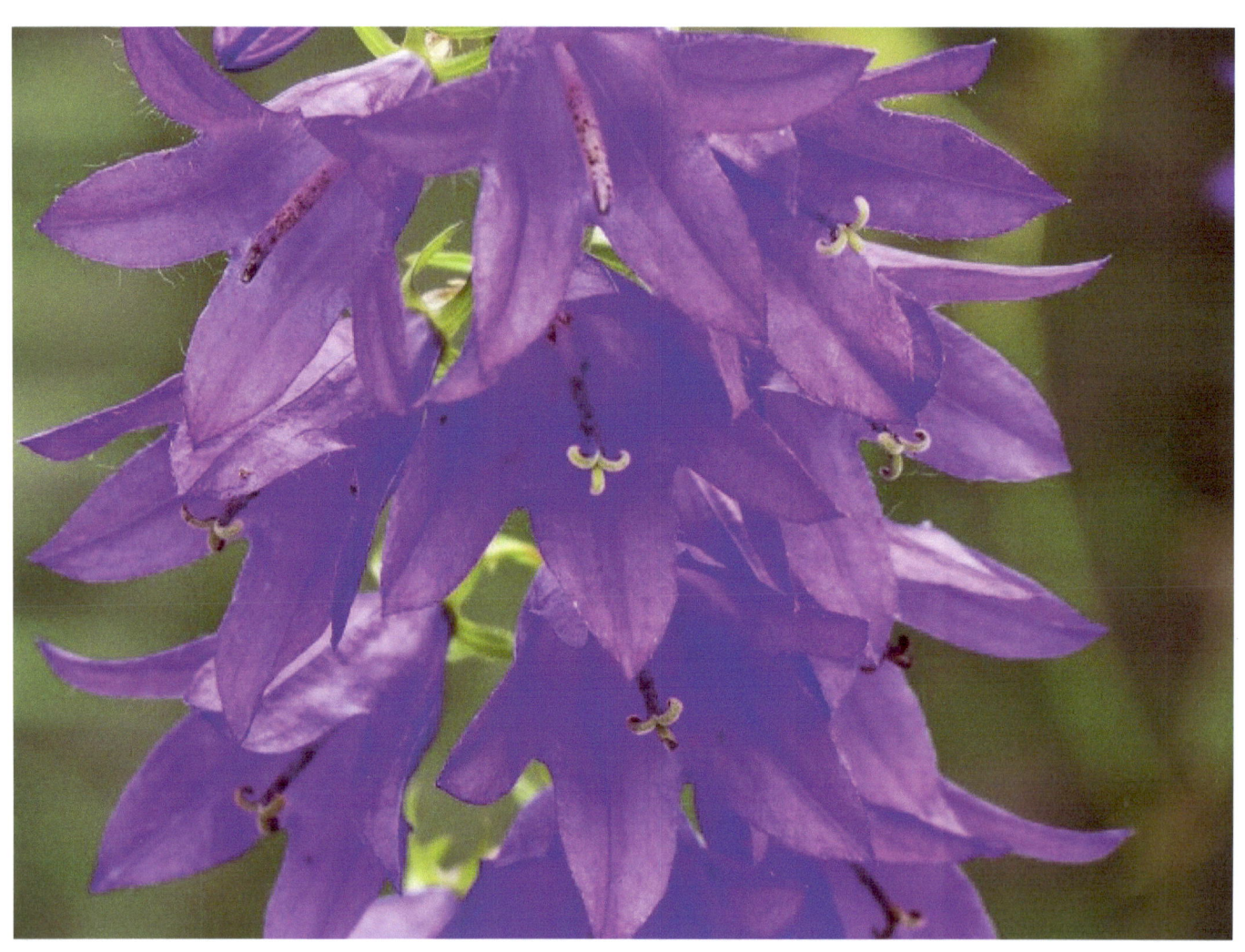

Beautiful flowers in my garden

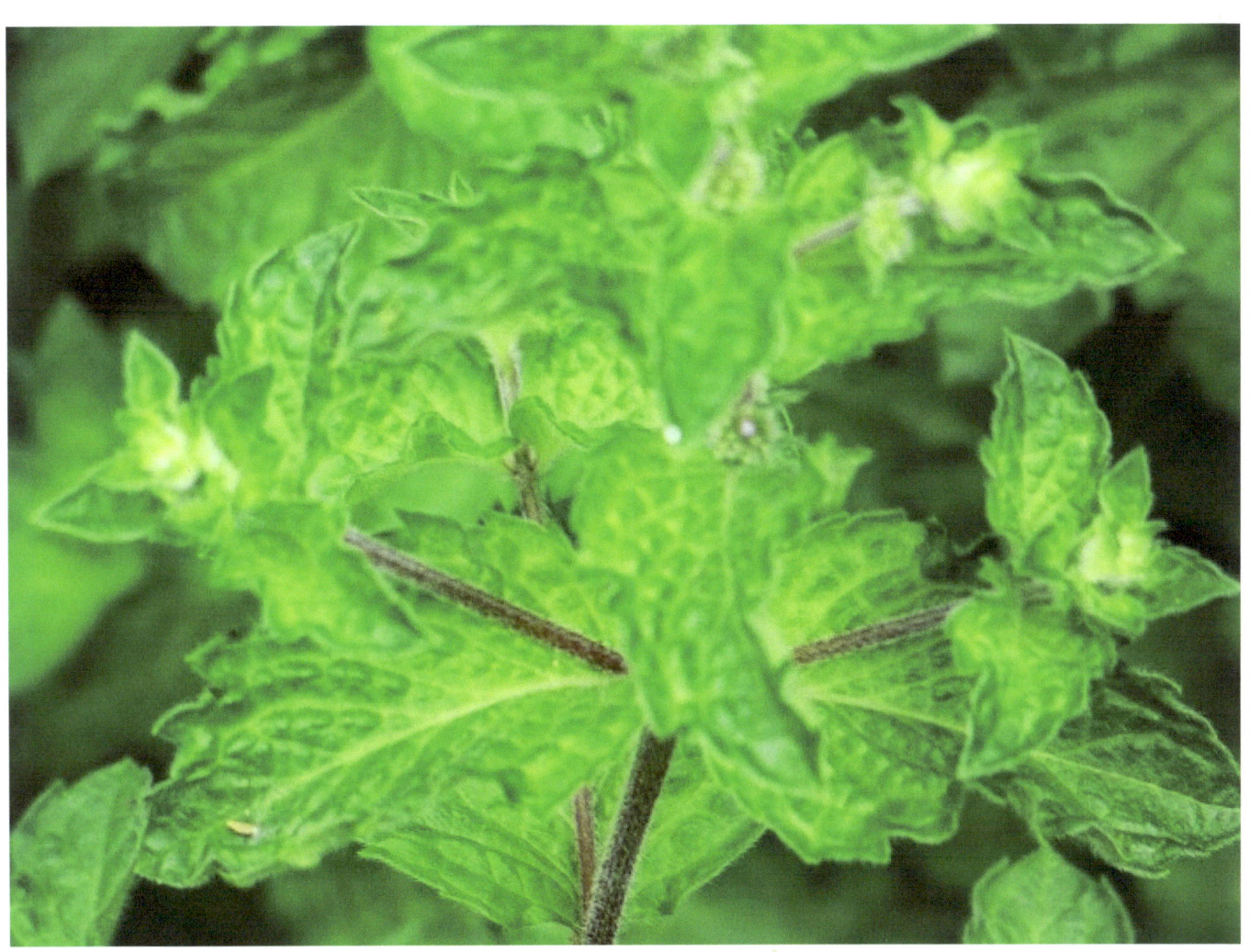

Lemon mint in my garden

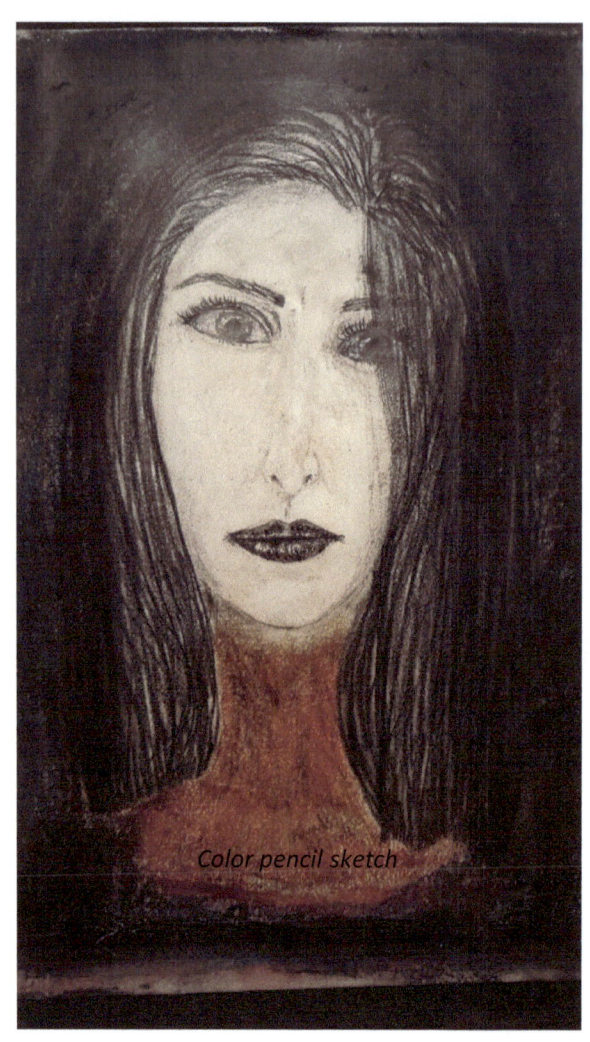
Color pencil sketch

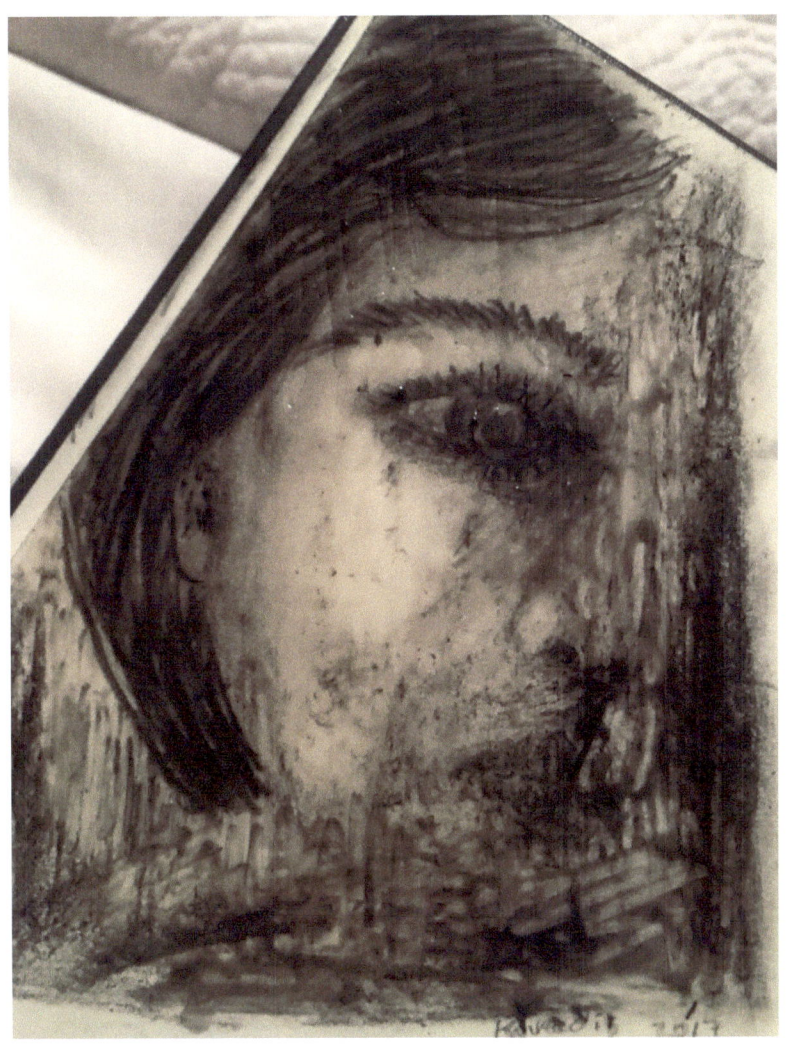

Black pencil sketch

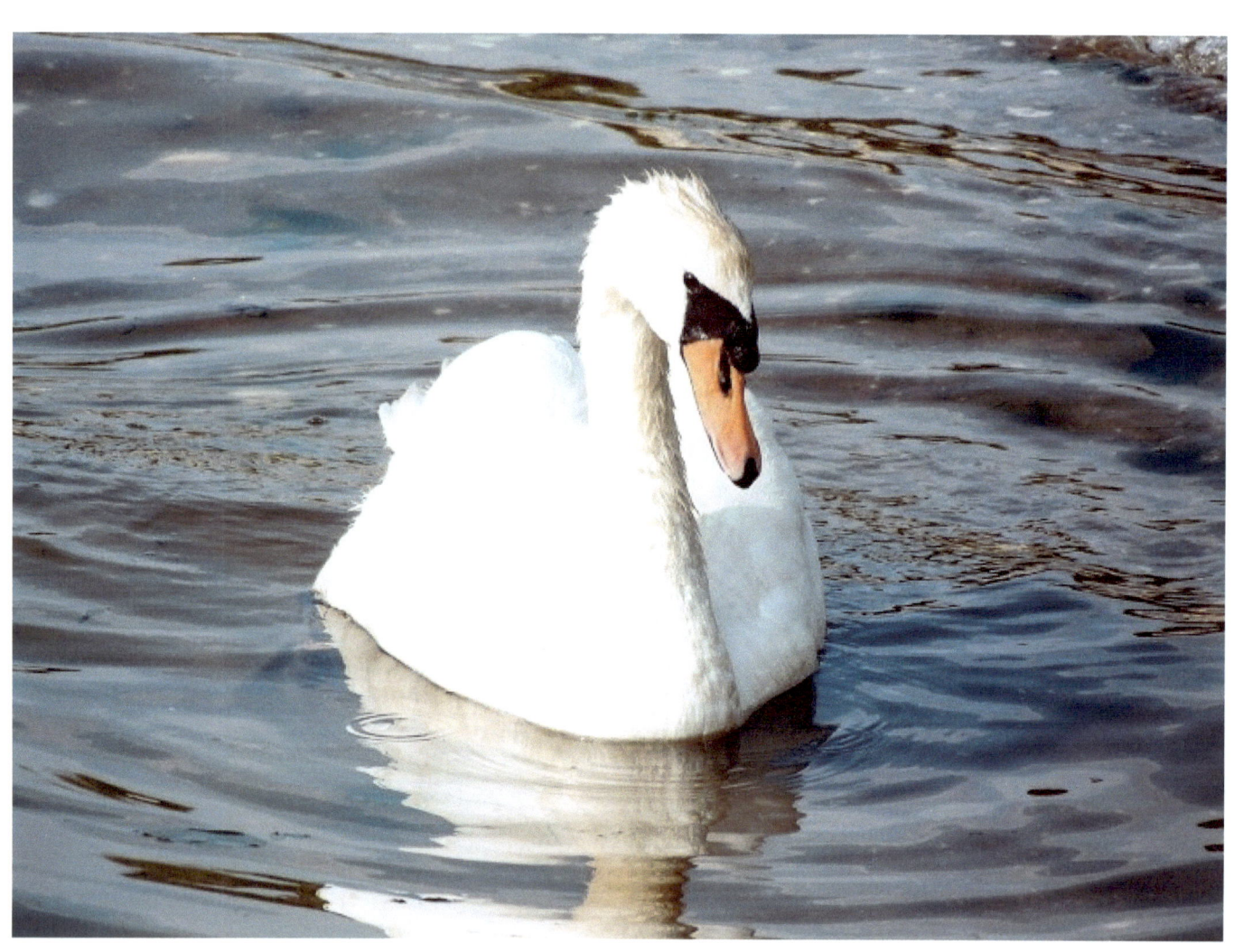

A swan passing by in Cranston RI, USA

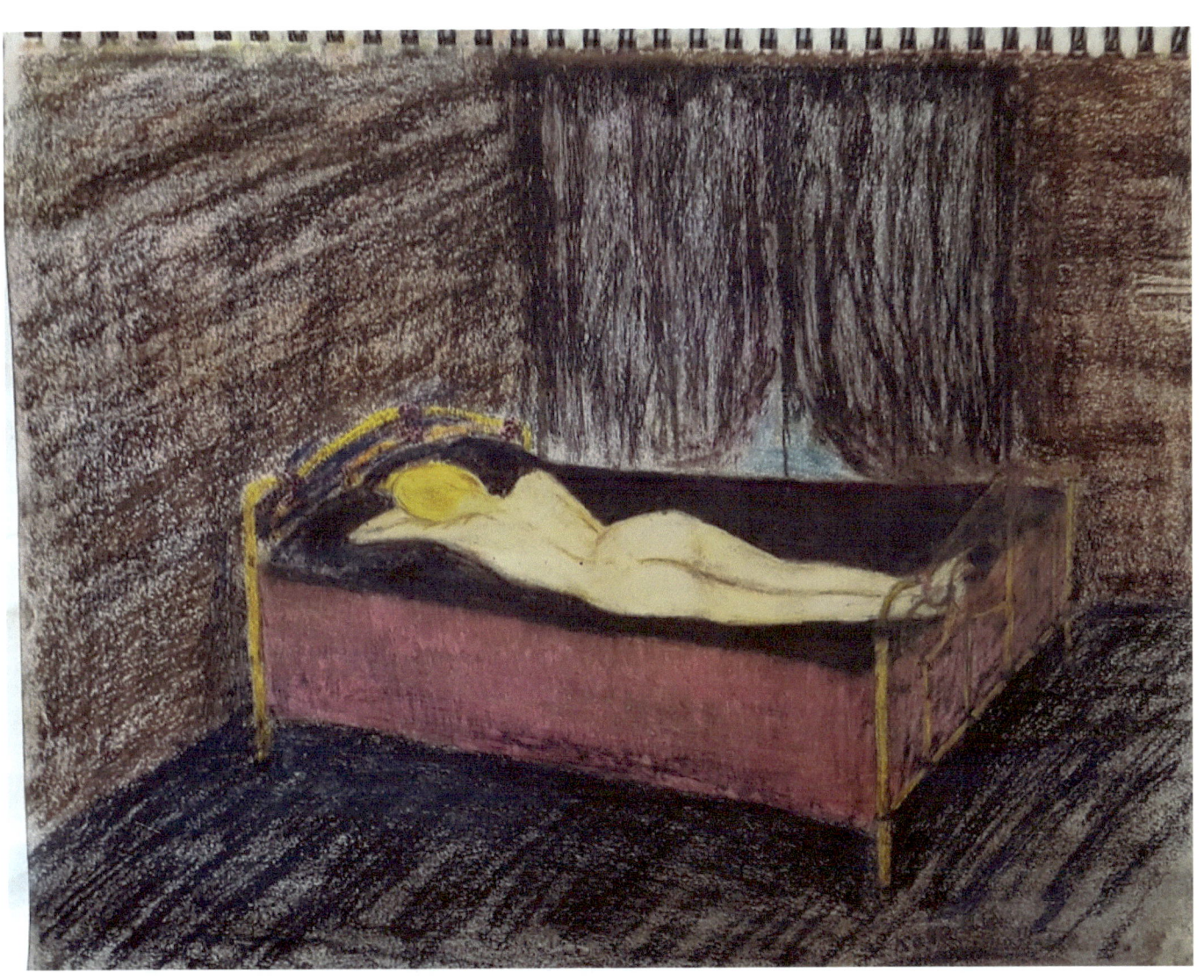

Color pencil sketch

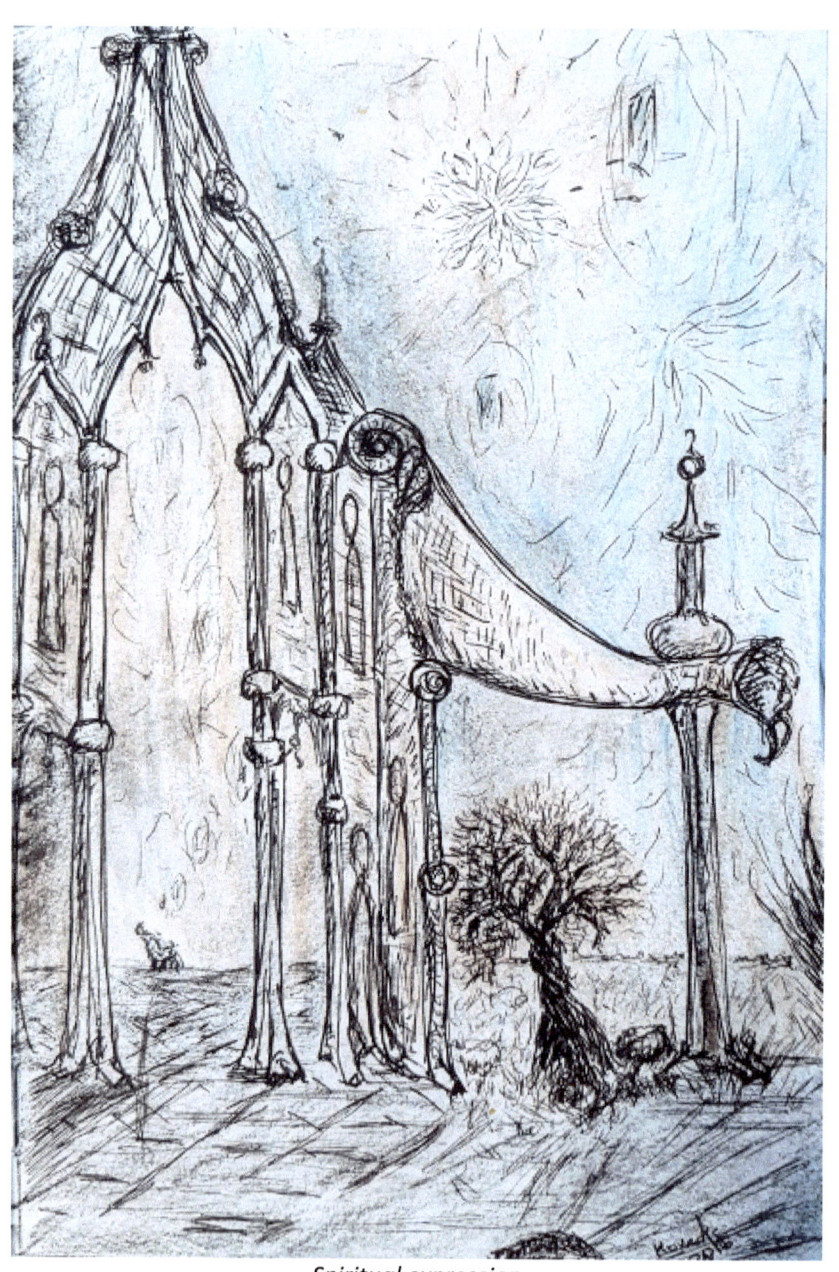
Spiritual expression

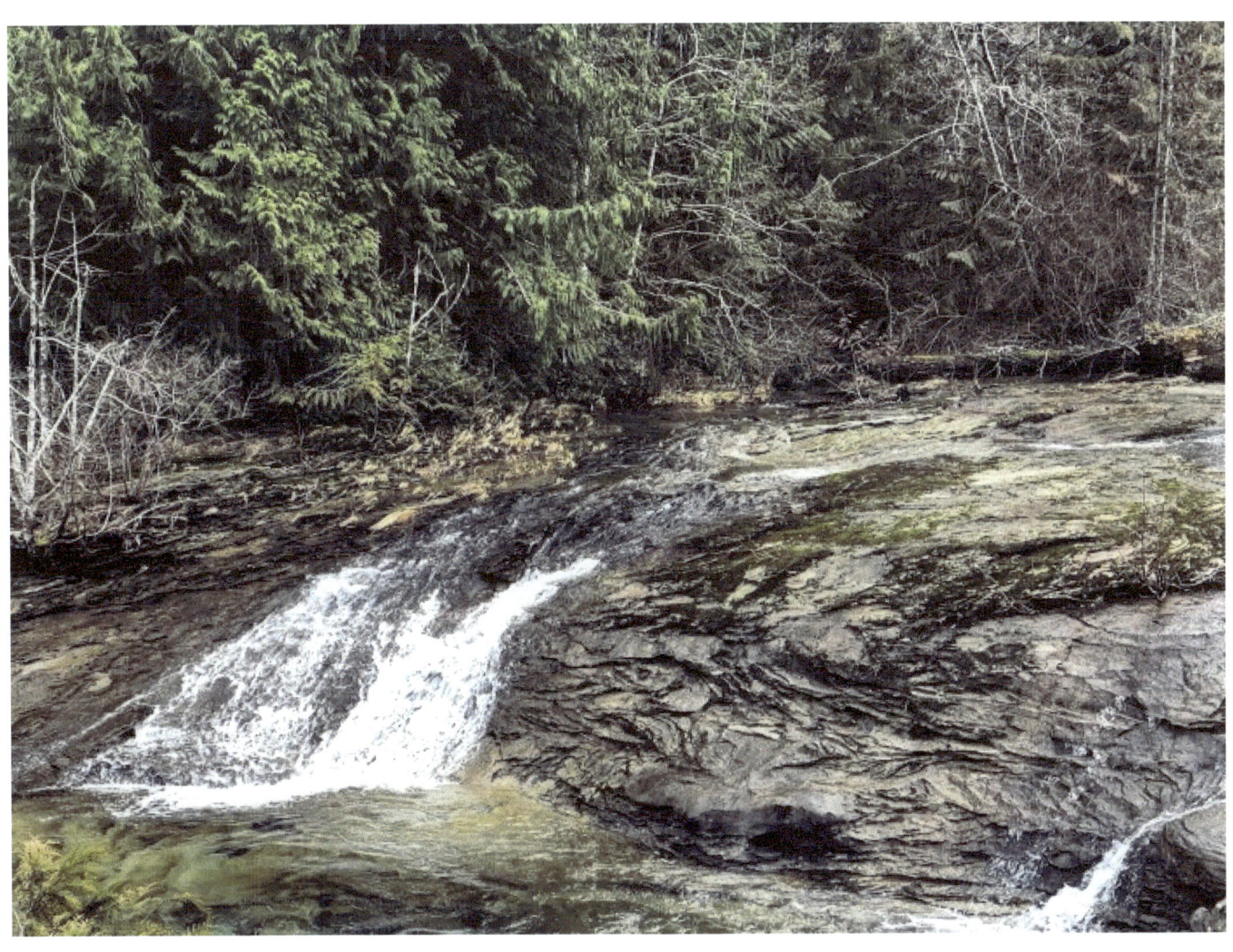

Beautiful Vancouver island BC, Canada

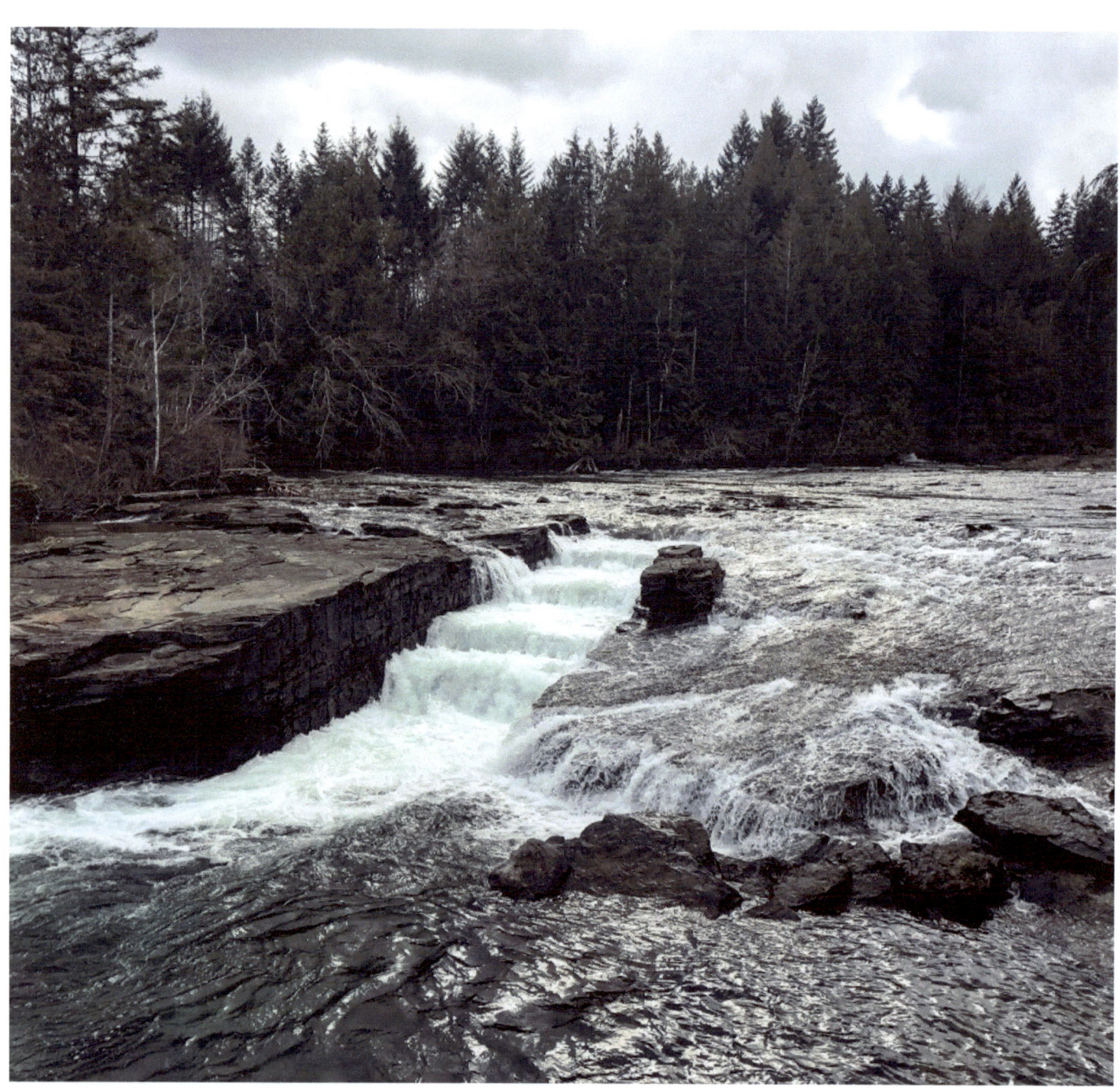

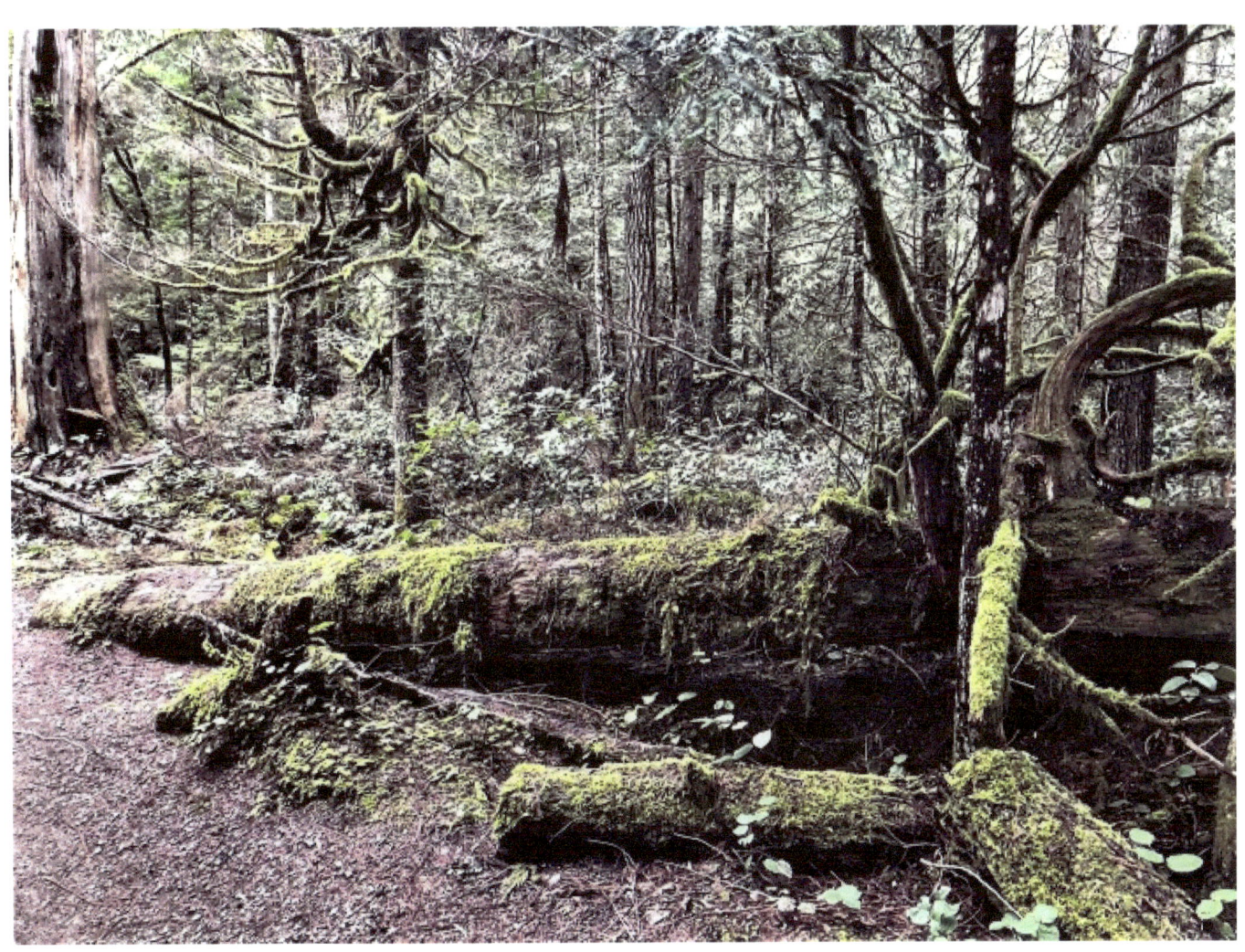

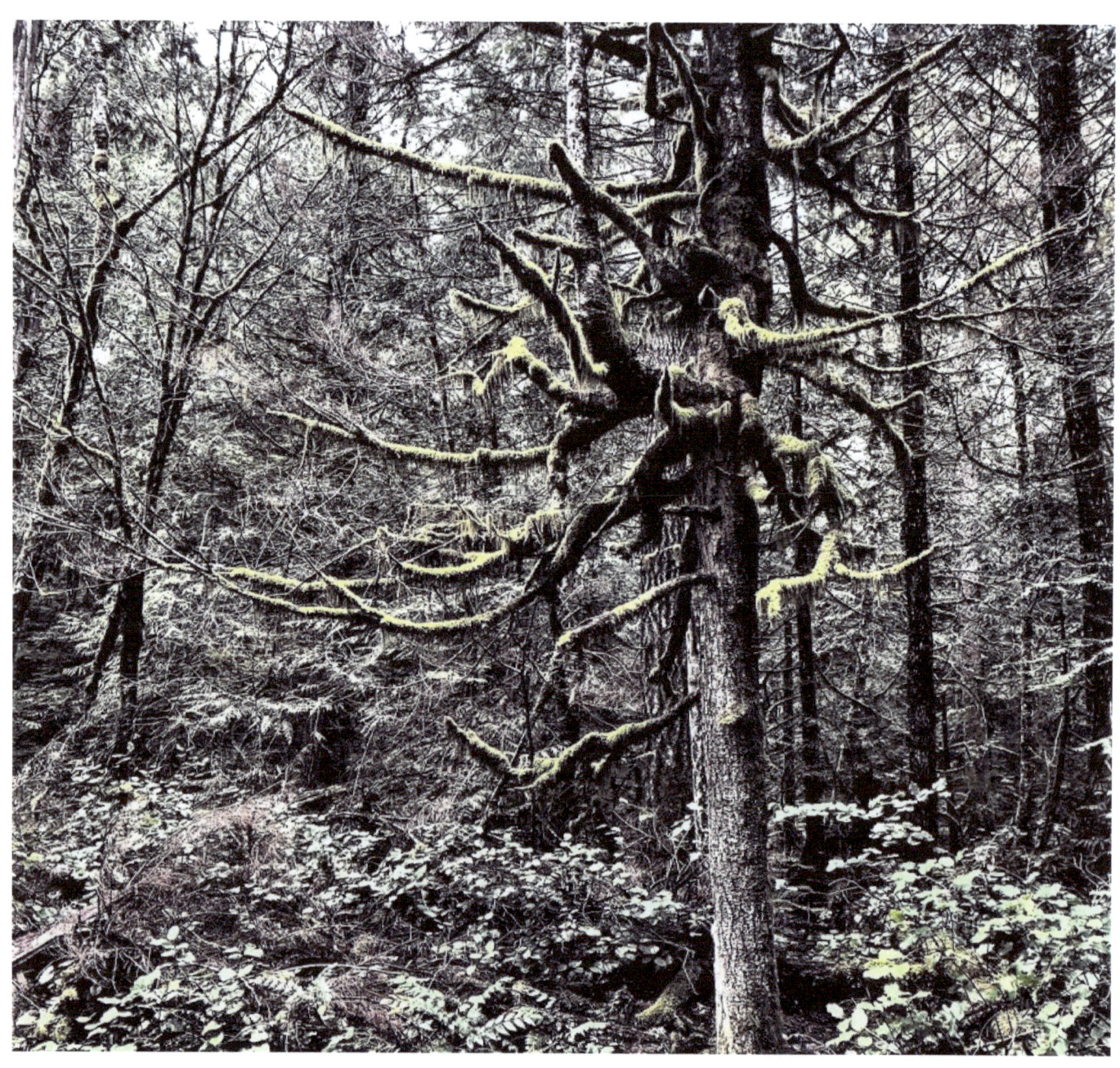

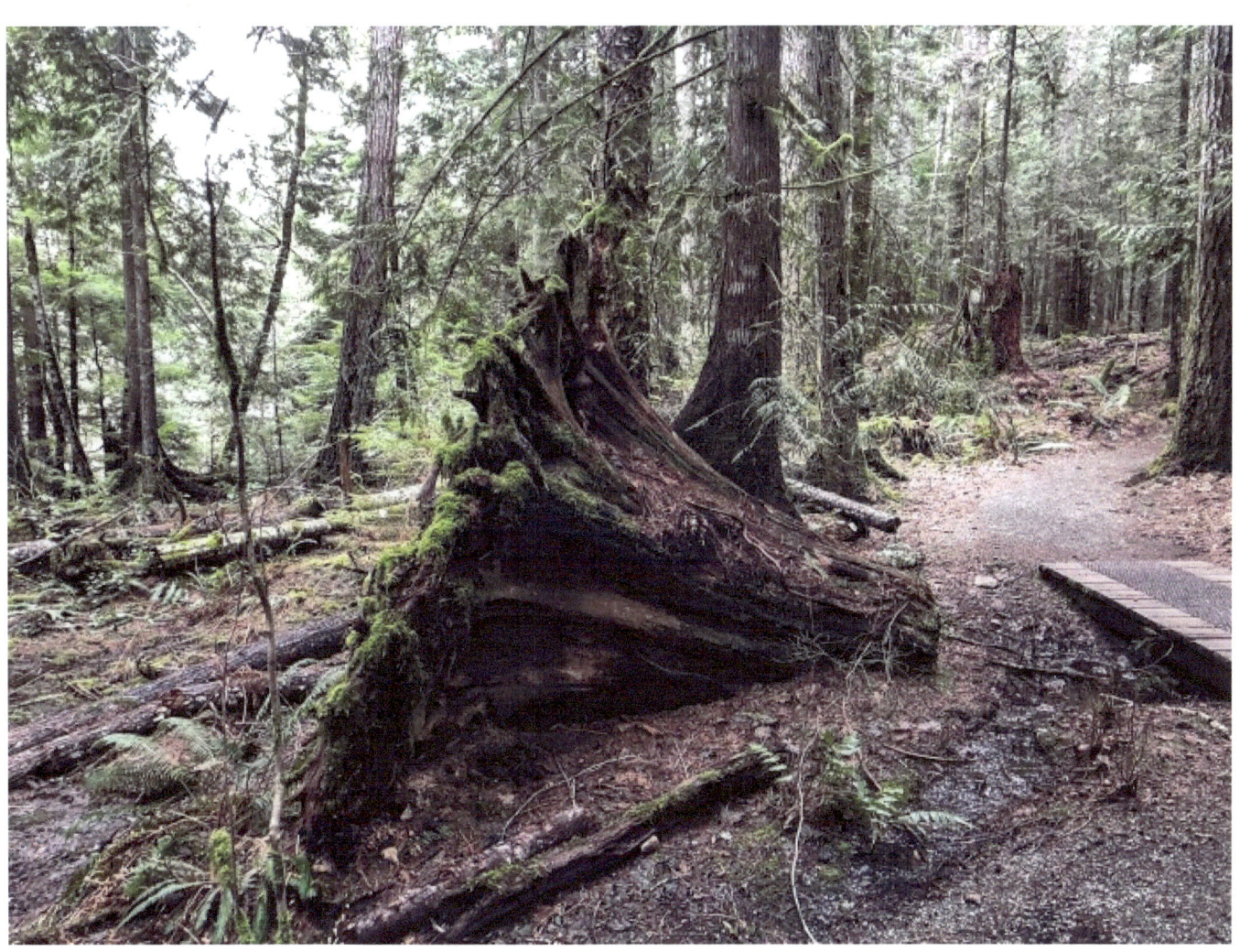

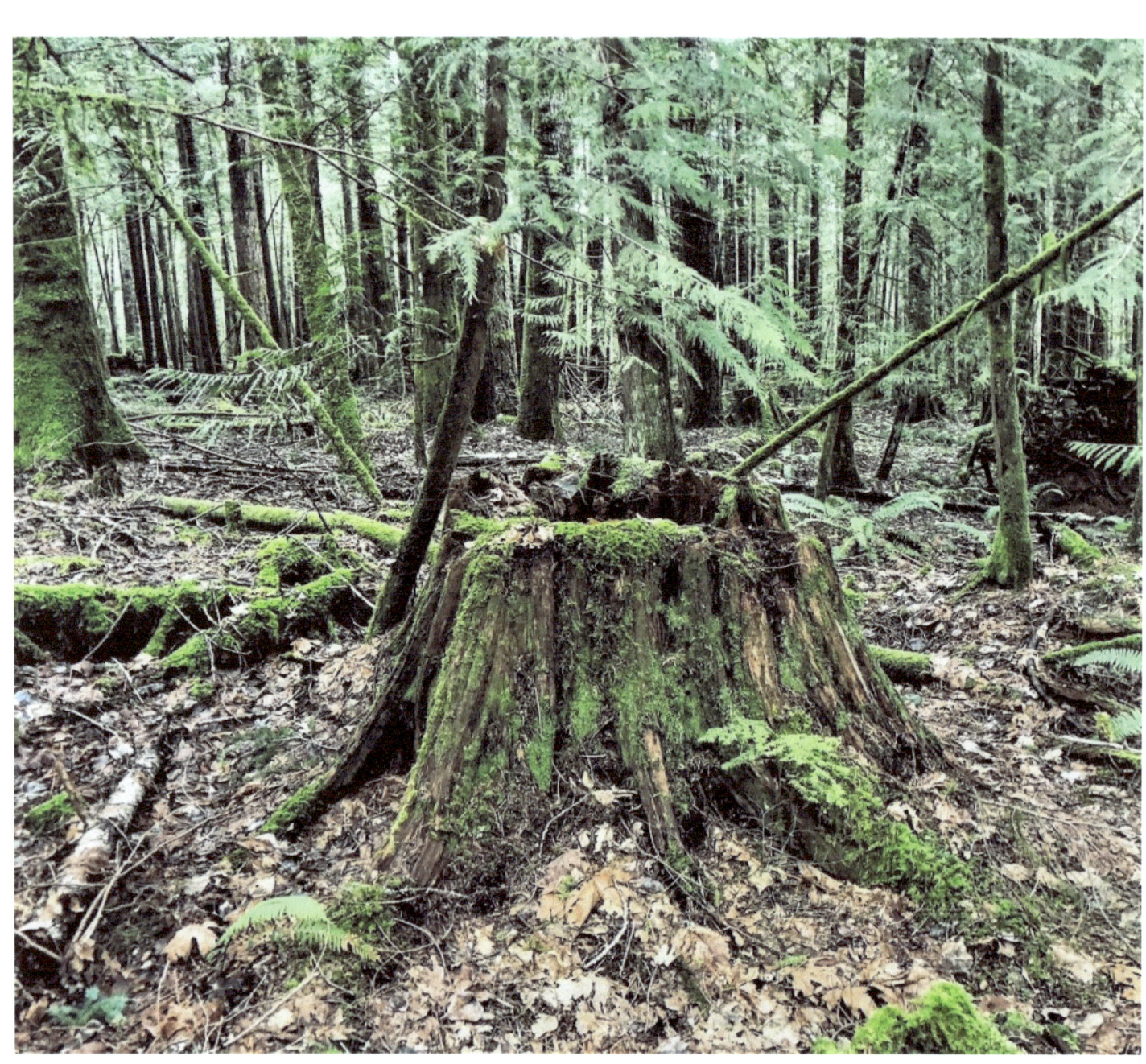

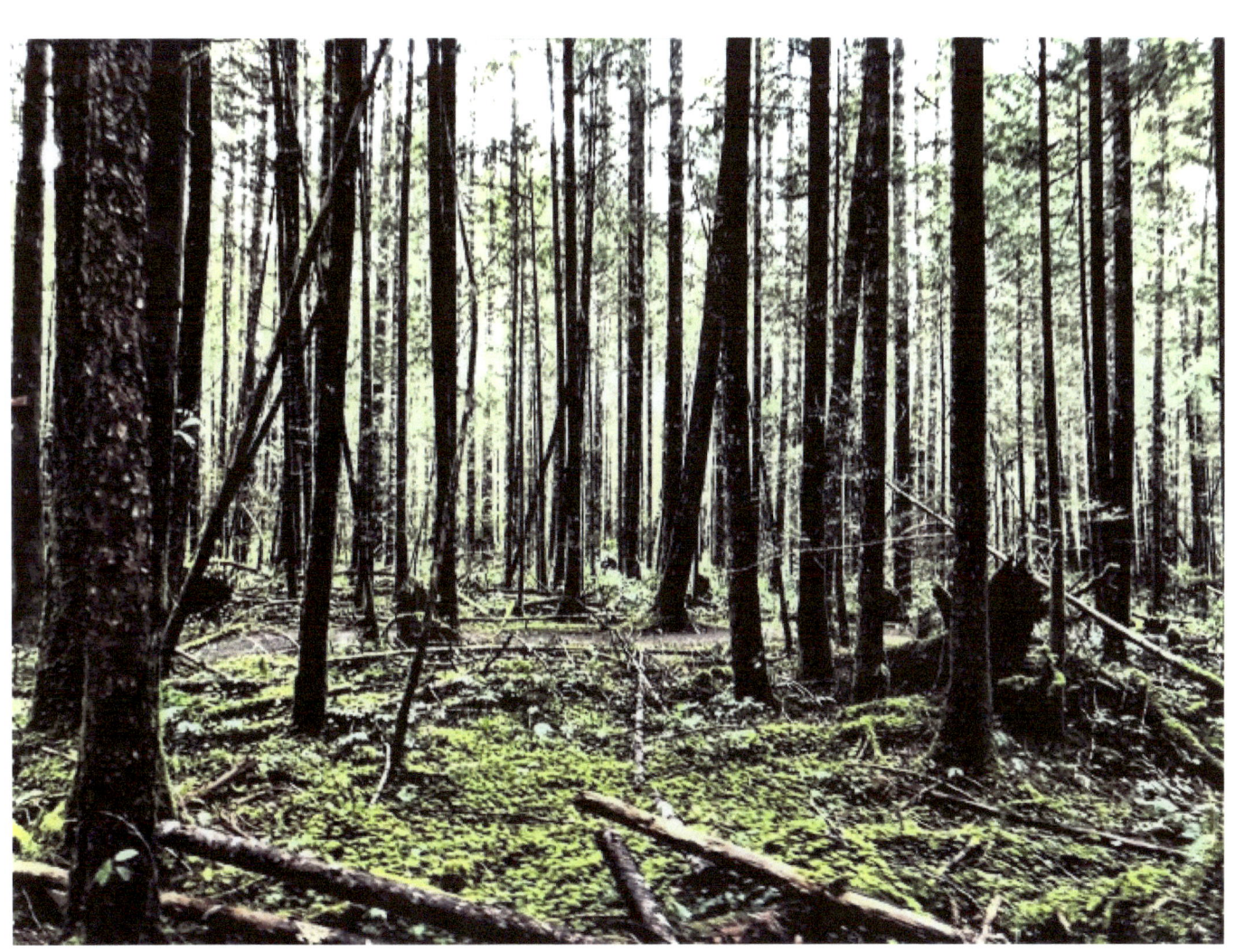

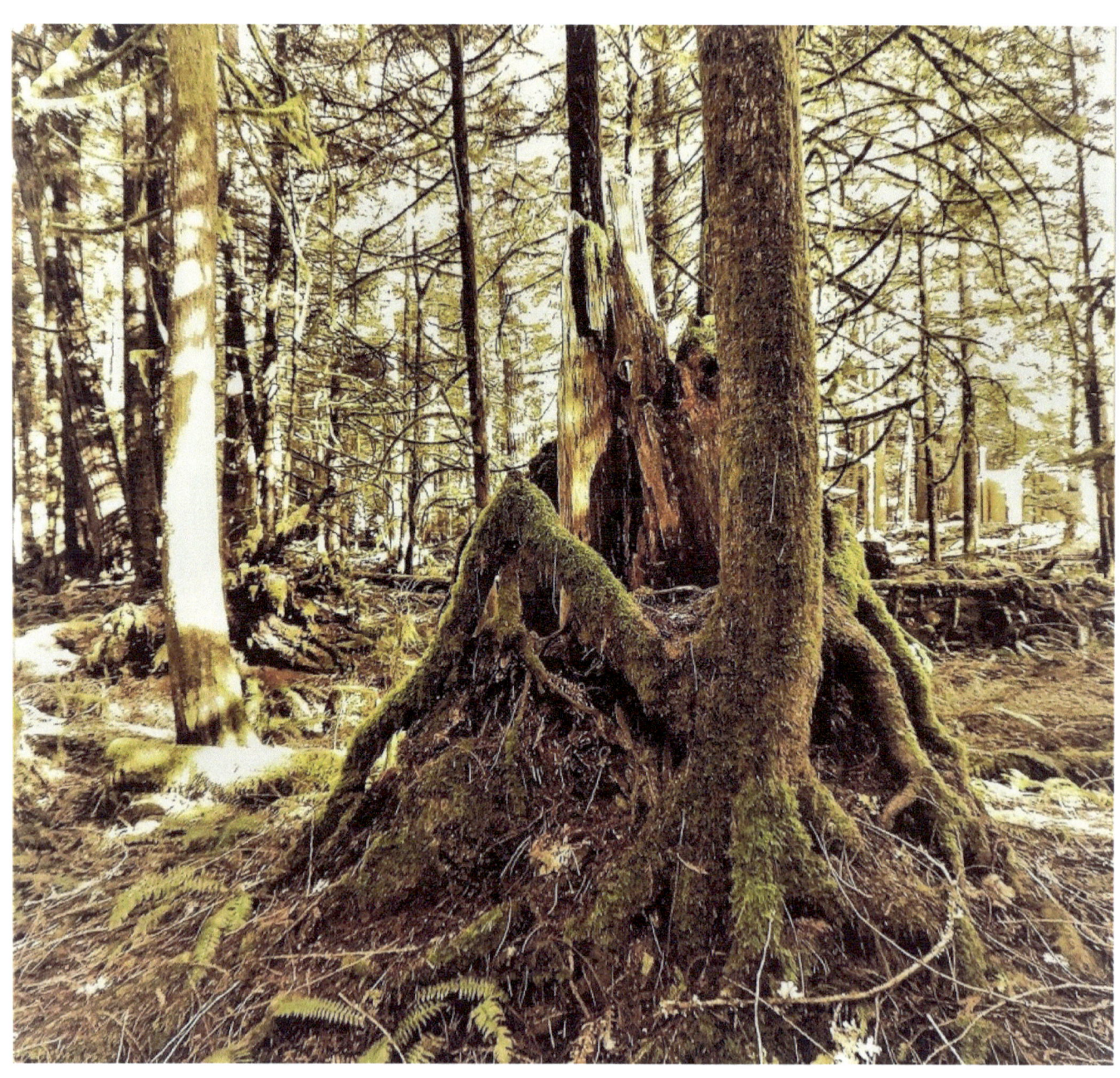

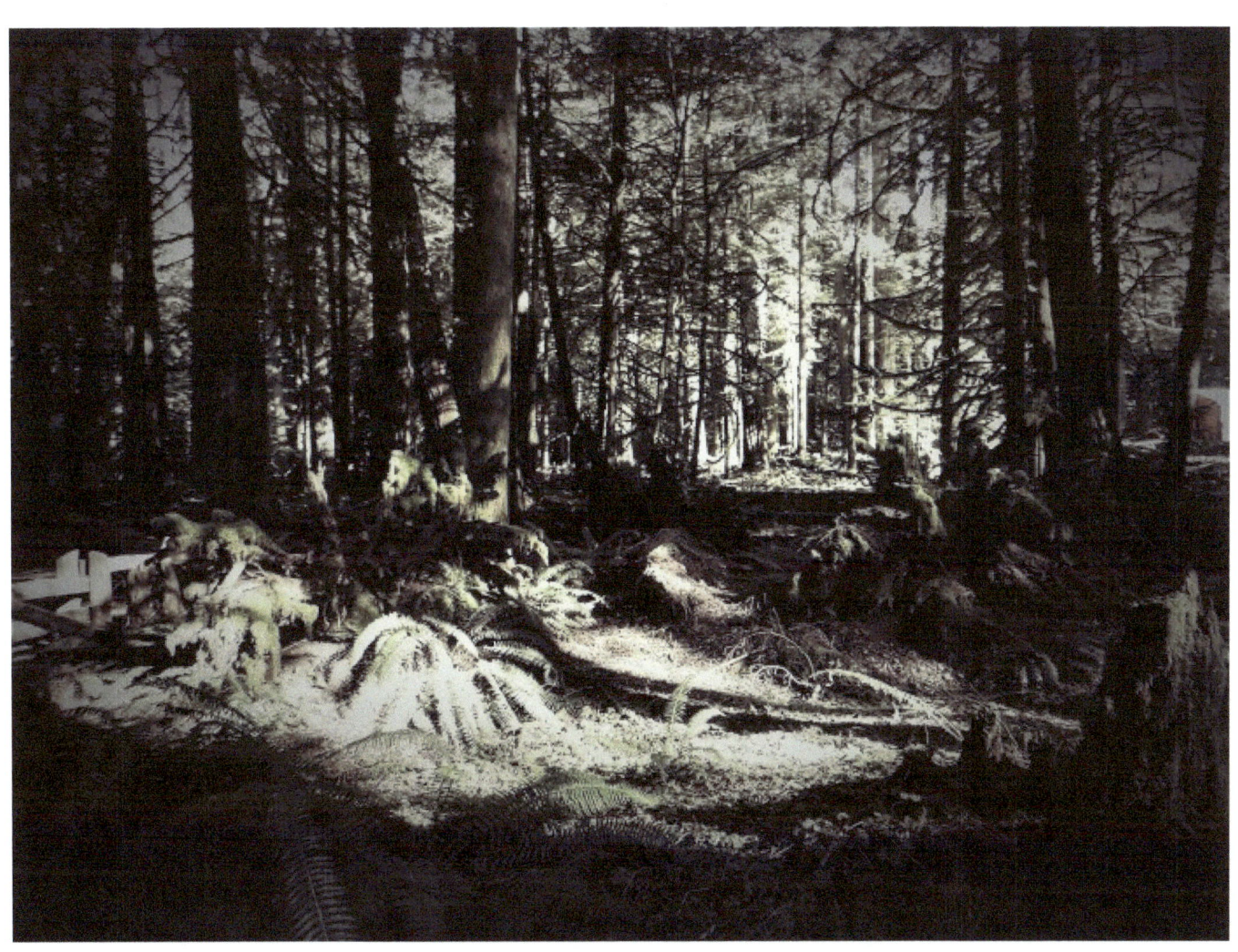

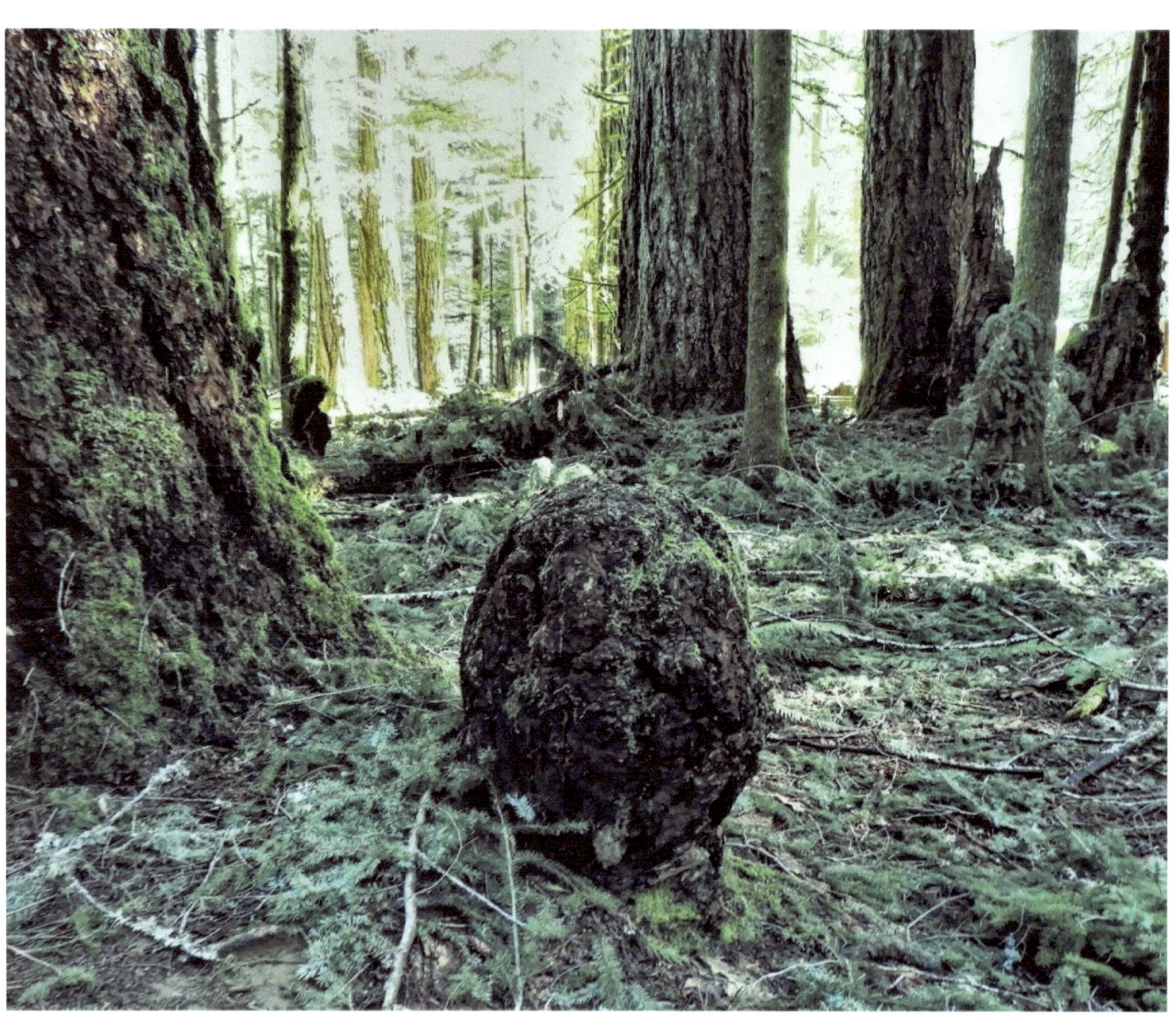

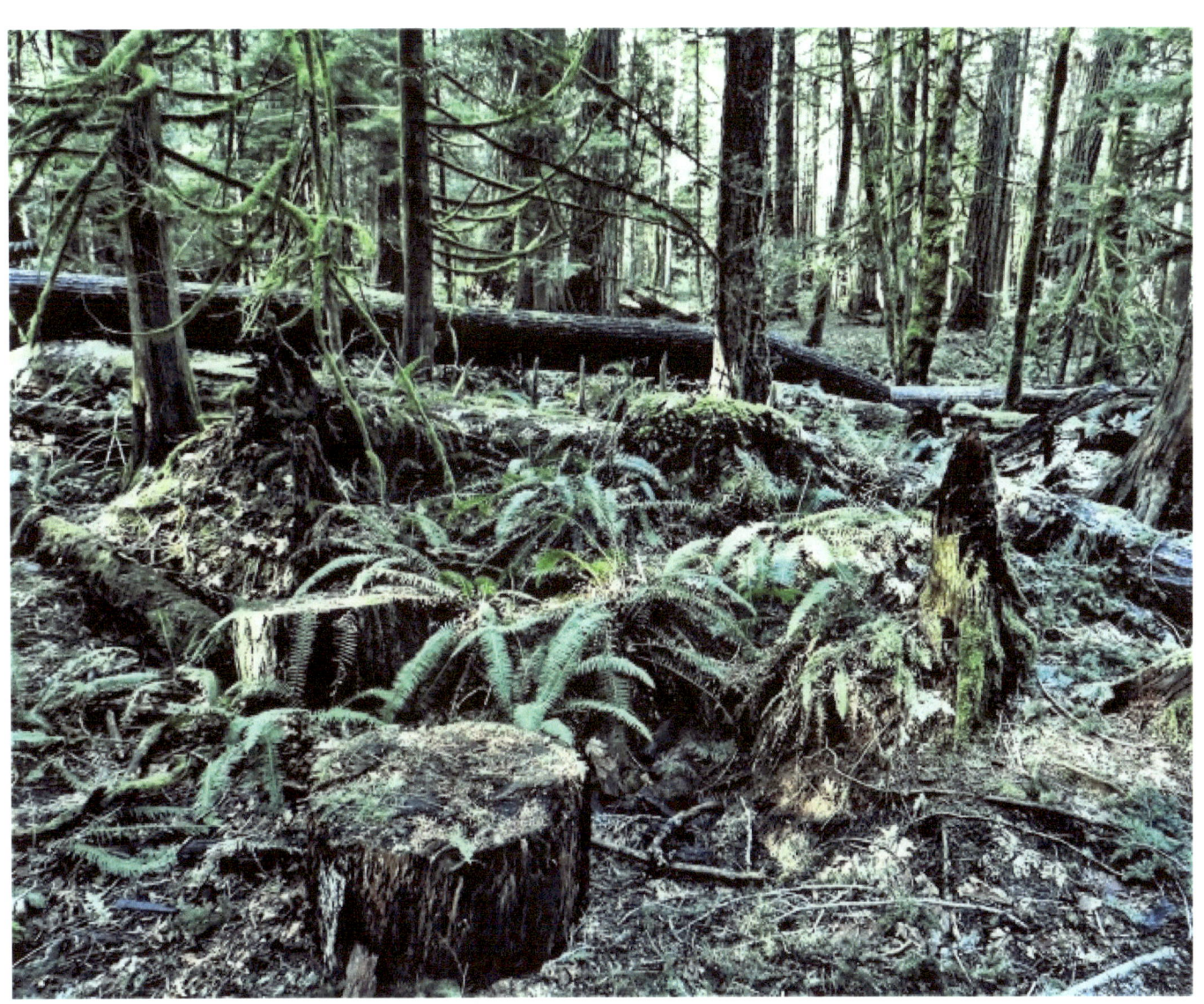

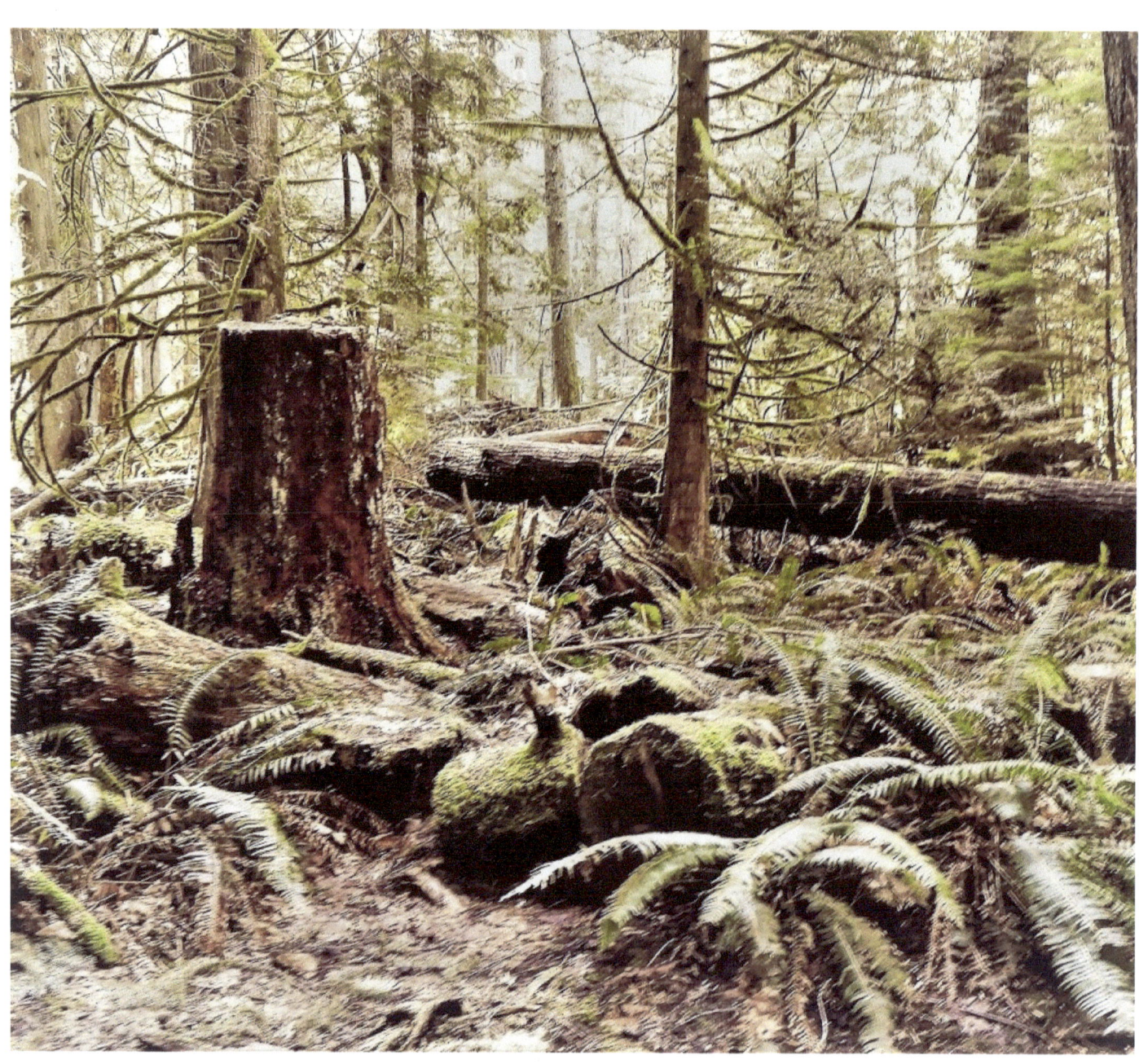

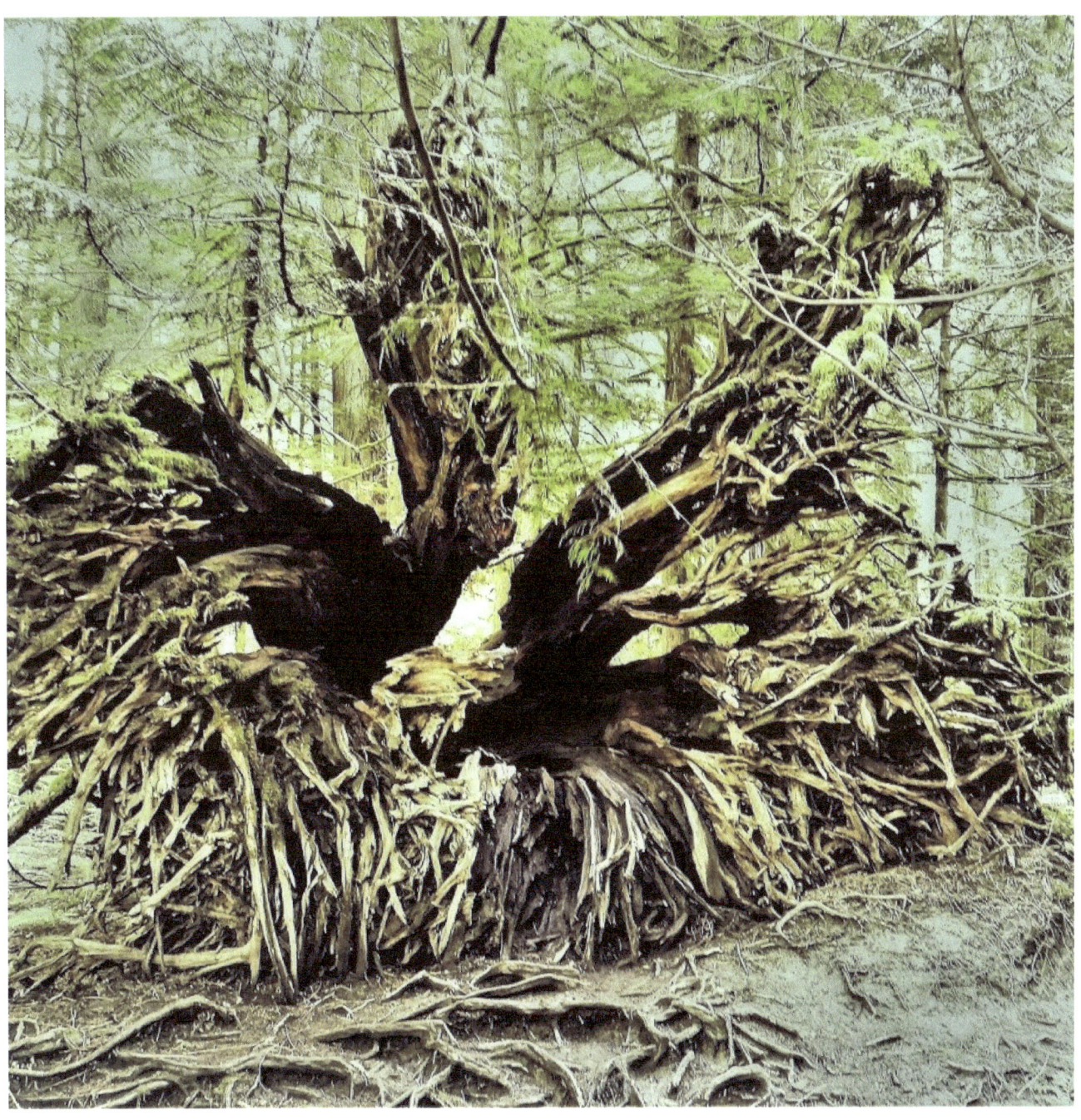

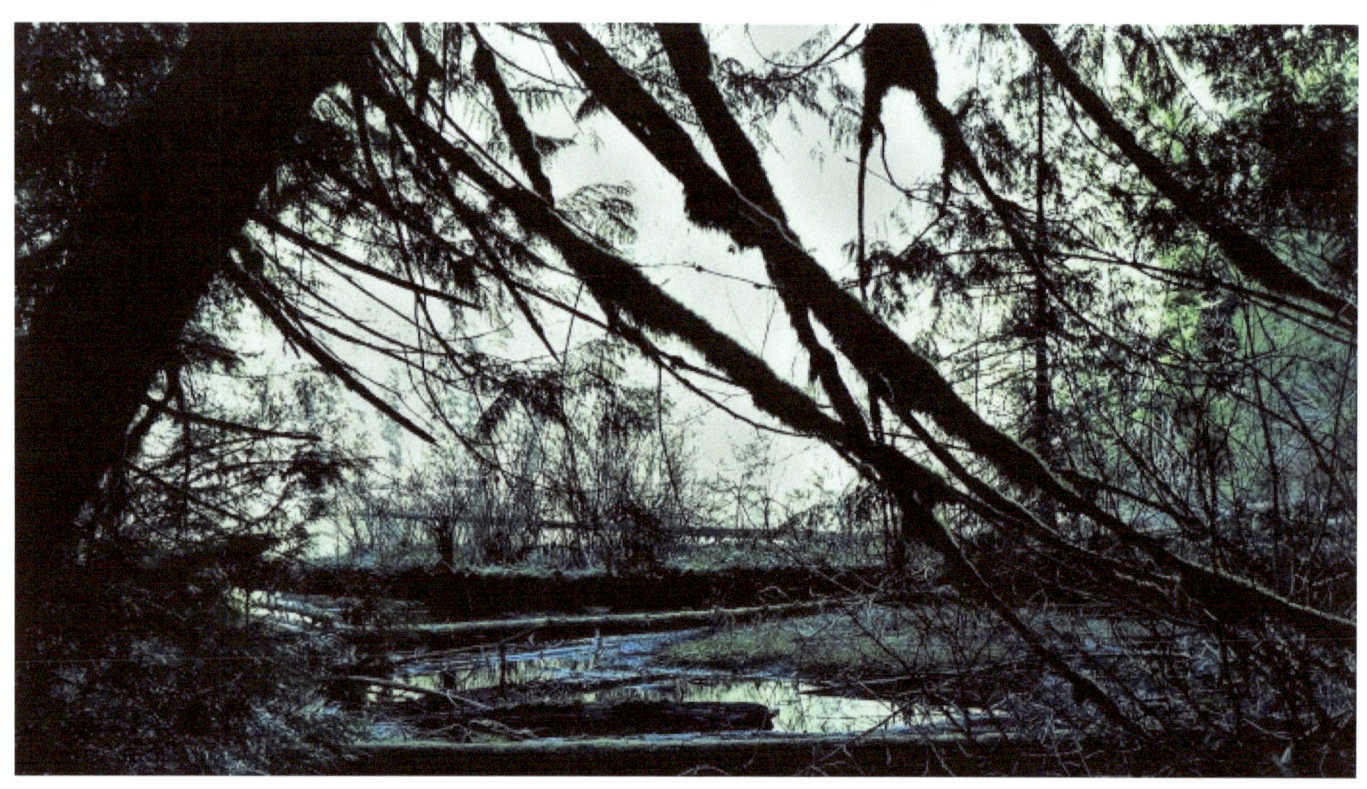

More pictures in beautiful Vancouver island, BC, Canada

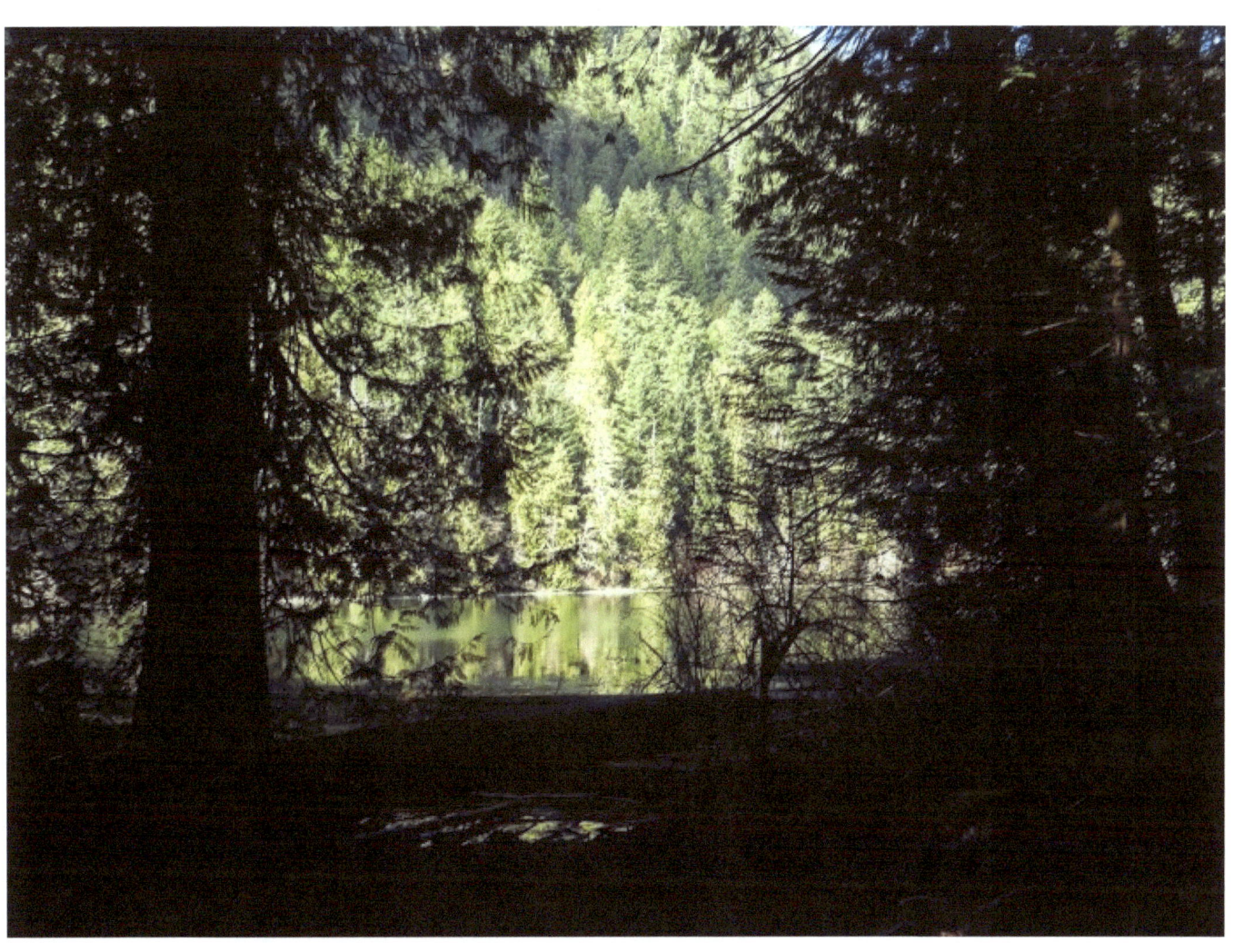

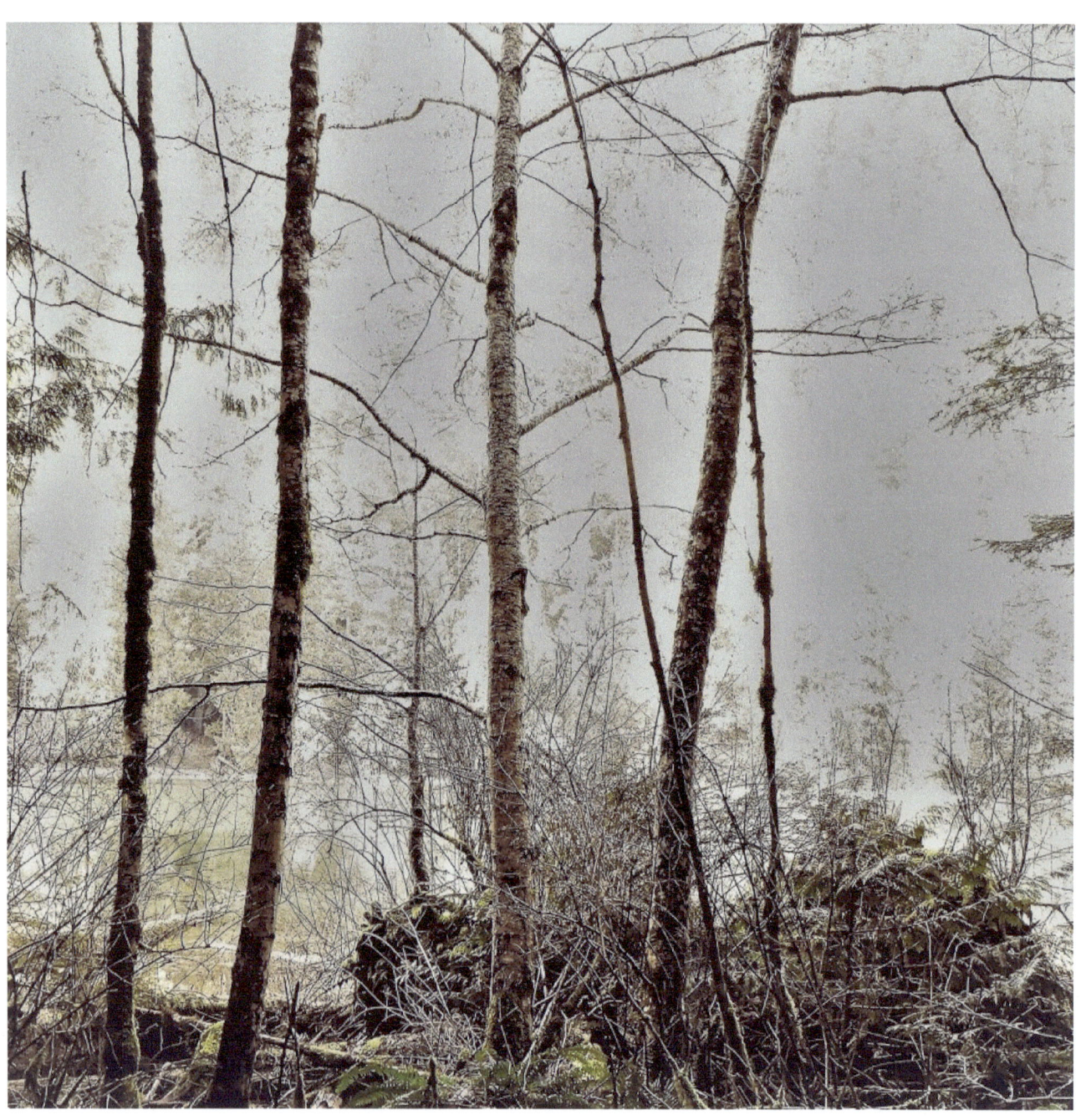

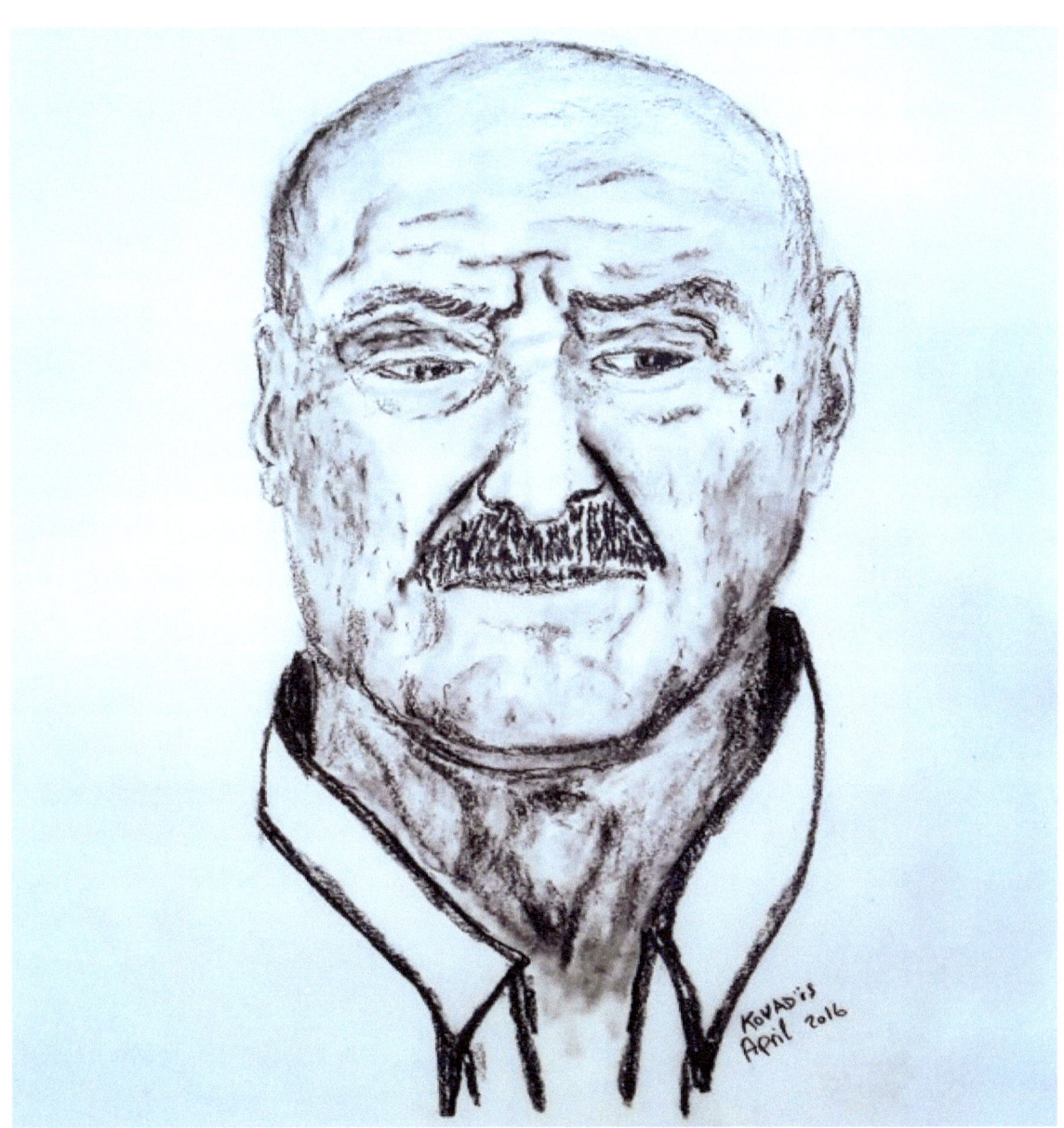

My dad, pencil sketch

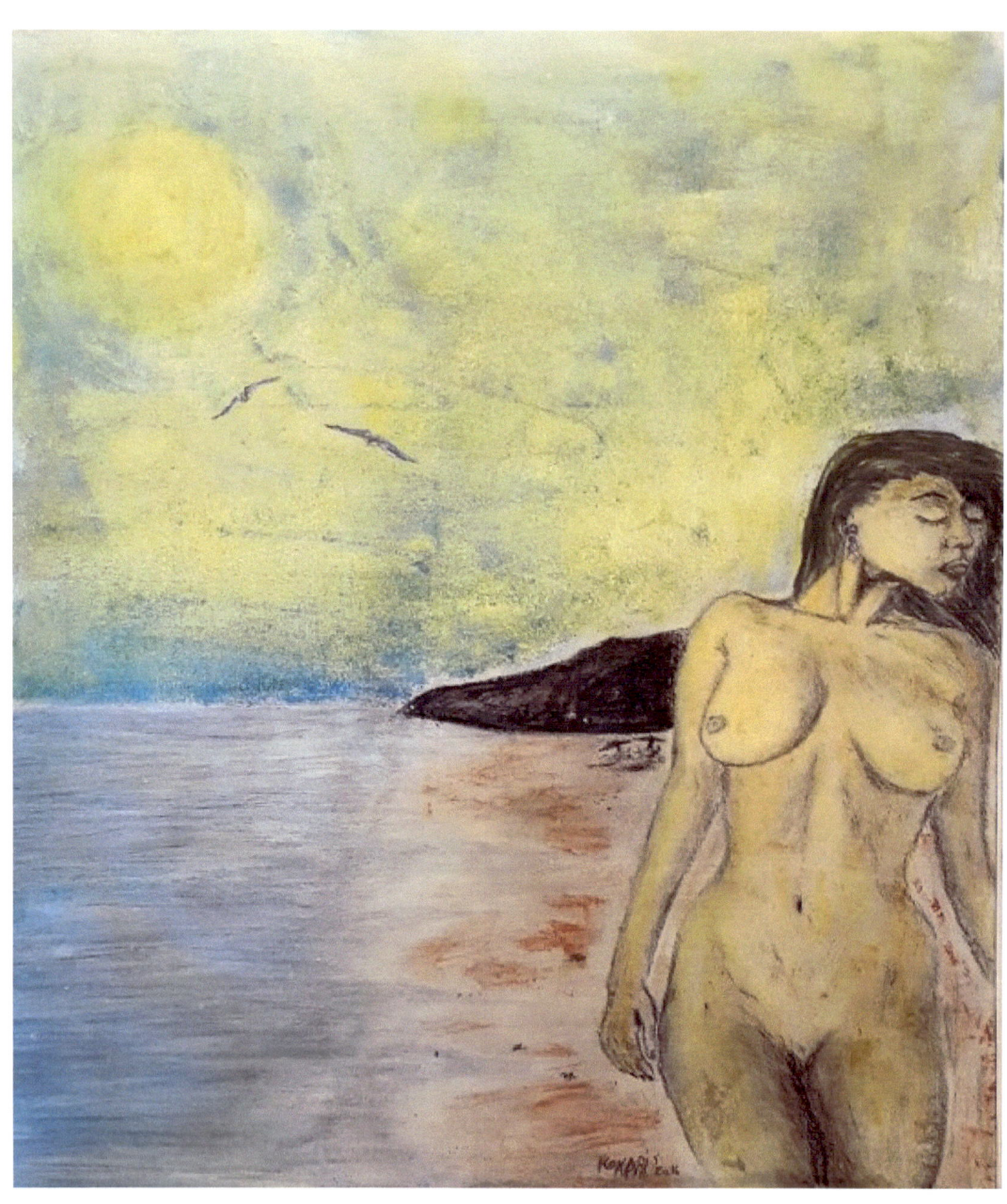

Color pencil sketch

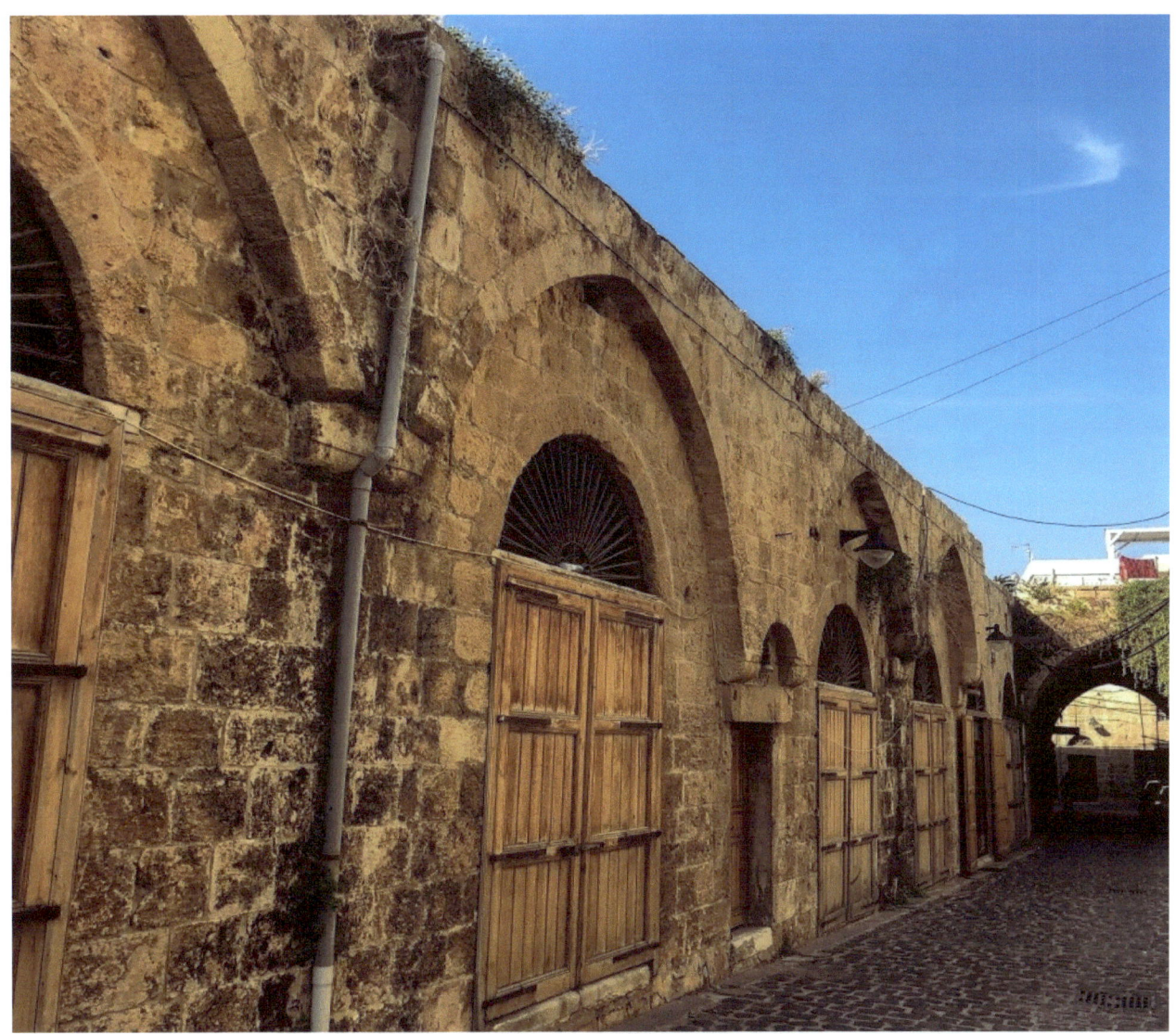
The old streets of Batroun, Lebanon. 2018 visit

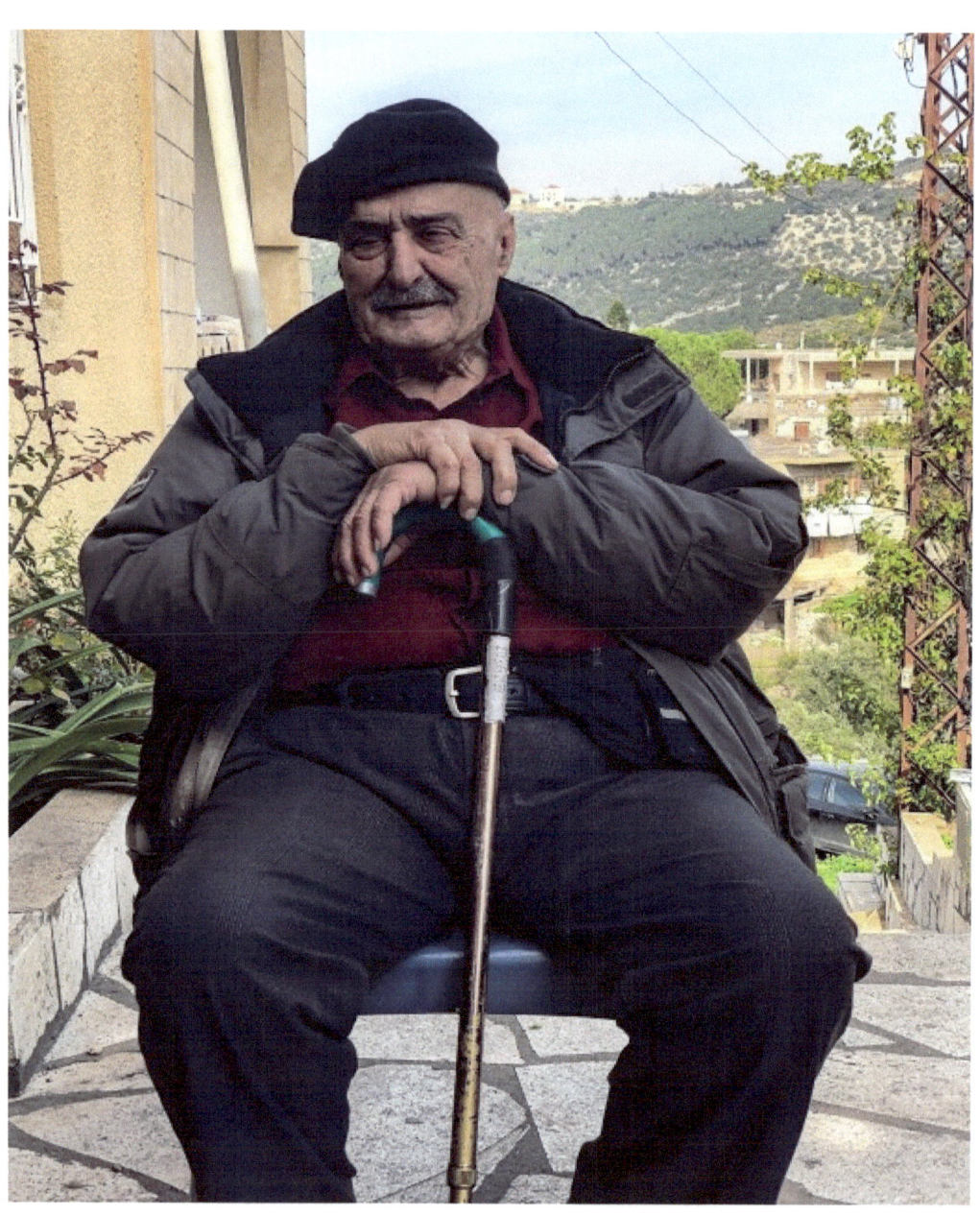

My dad happy to be visiting home after 35 years

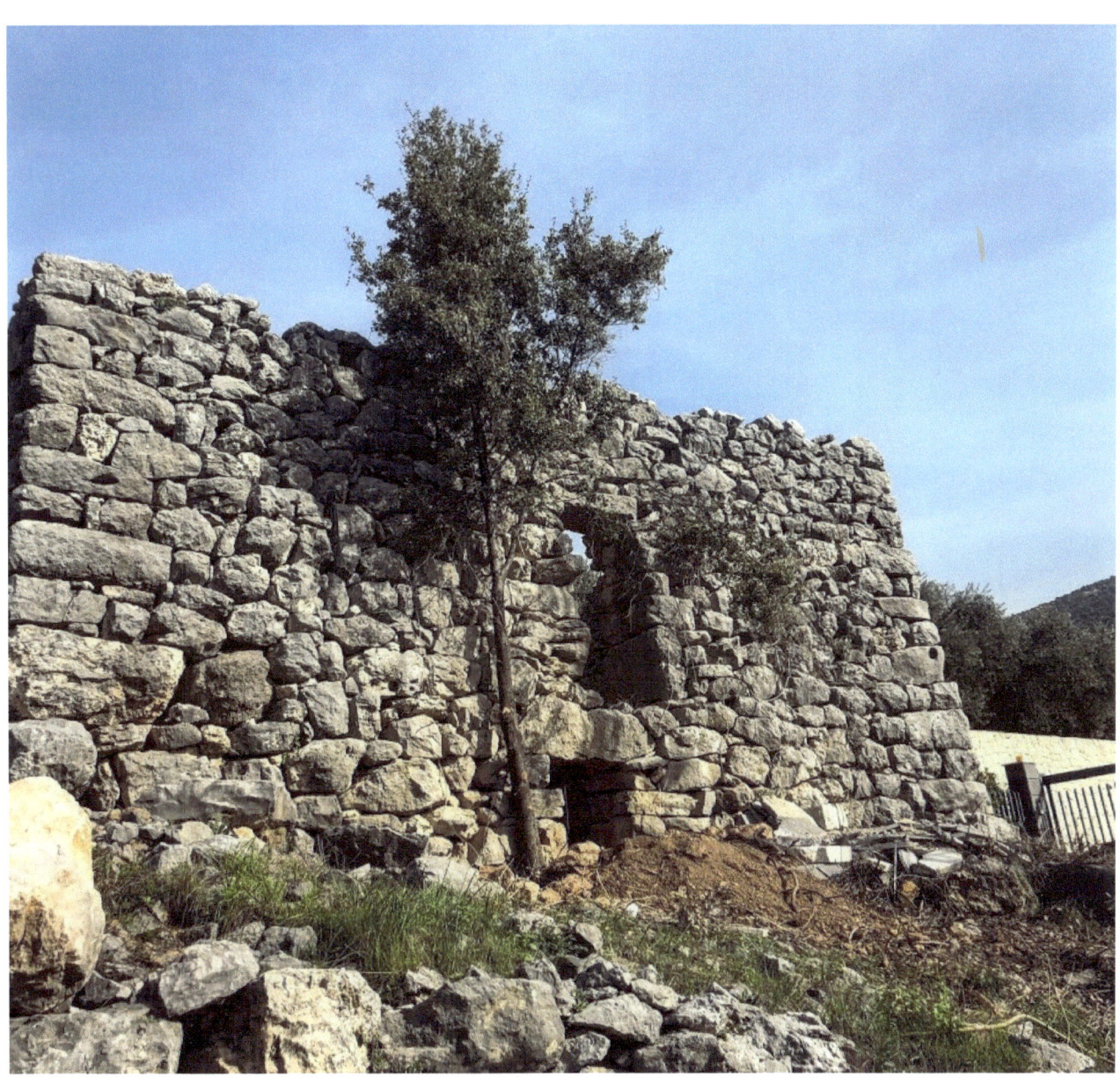

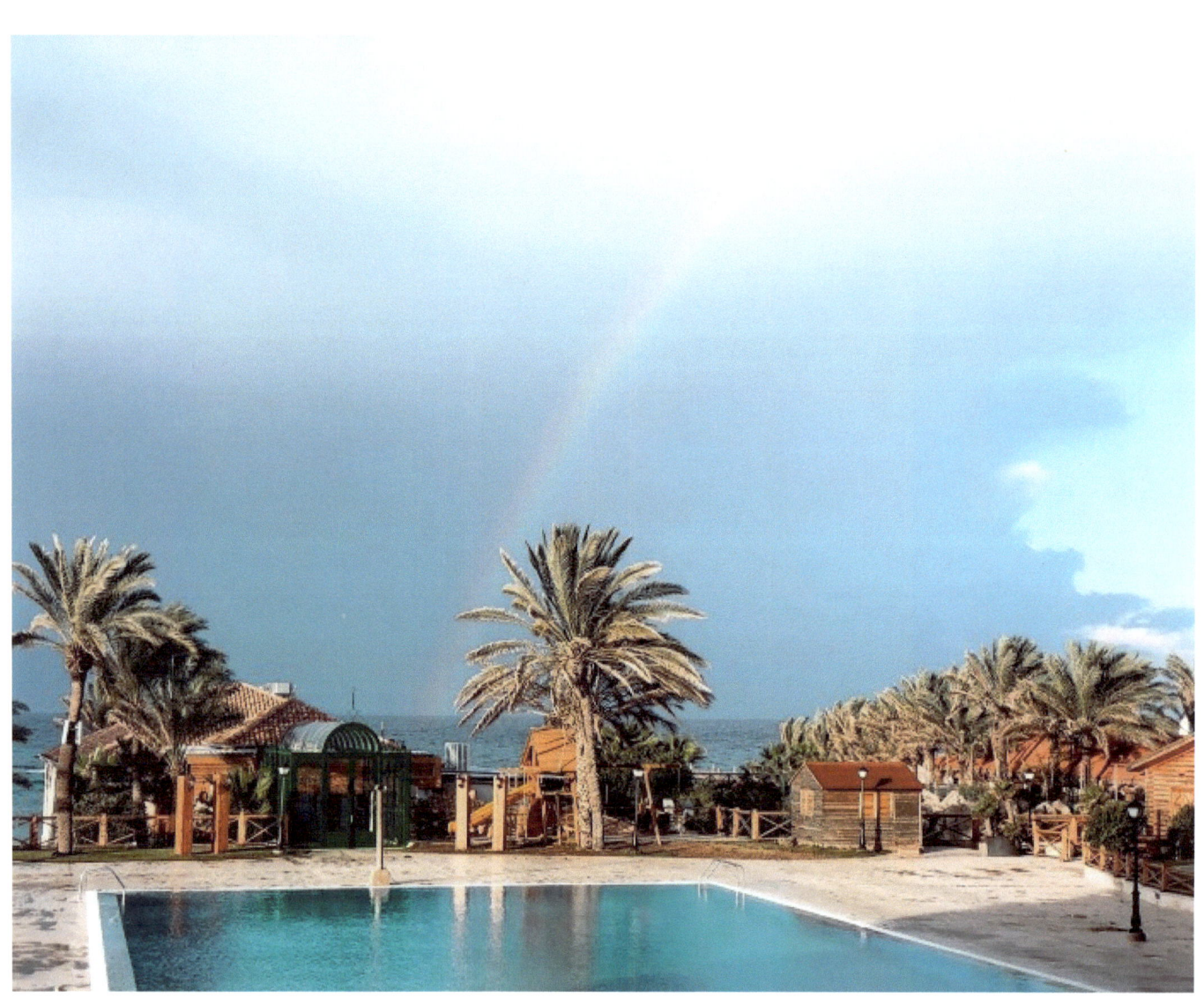

The view from My window While in Batroun Lebanon during my first visit there.

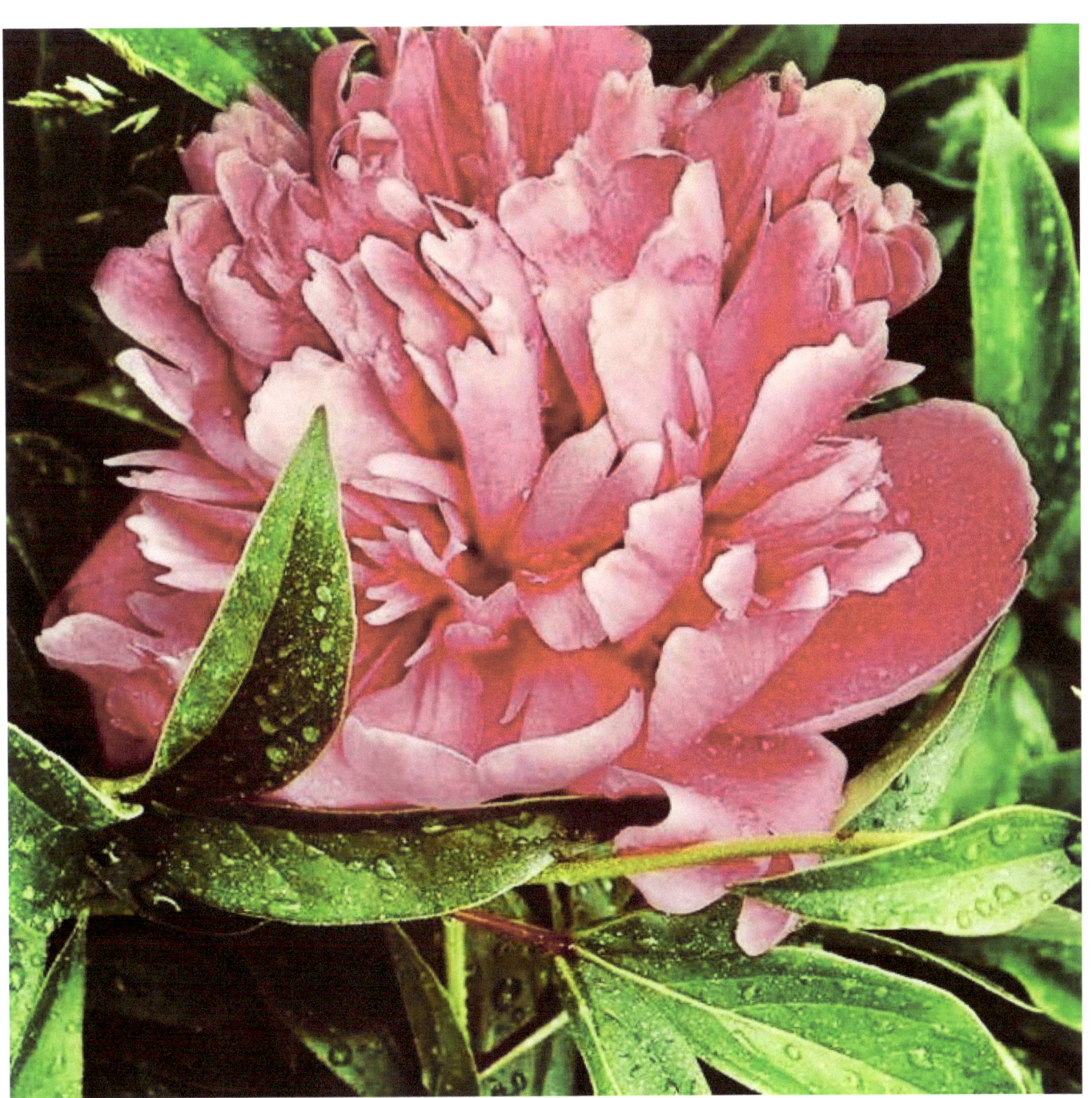

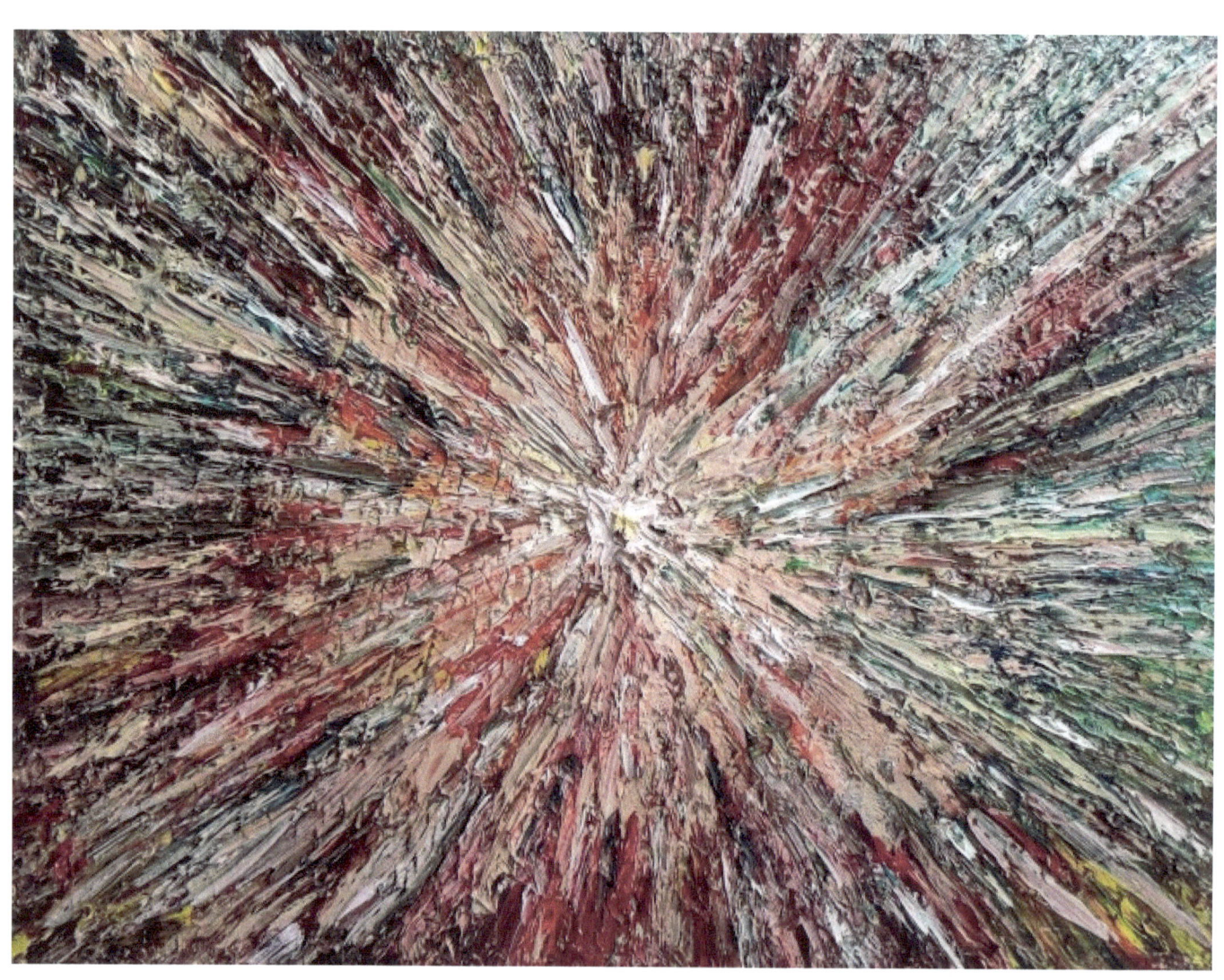
An explosion of color, oil on canvas

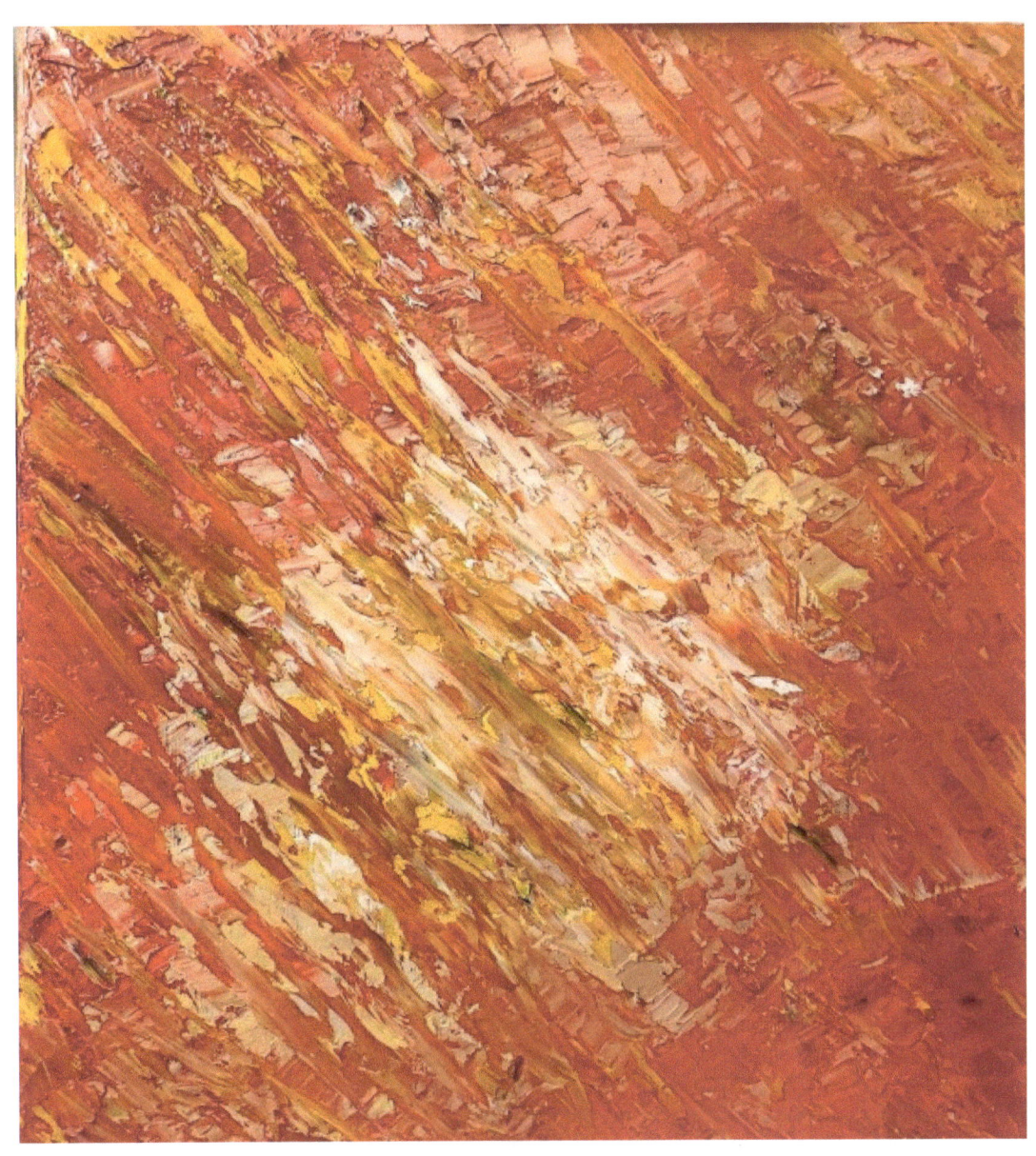

Oil on canvas color study

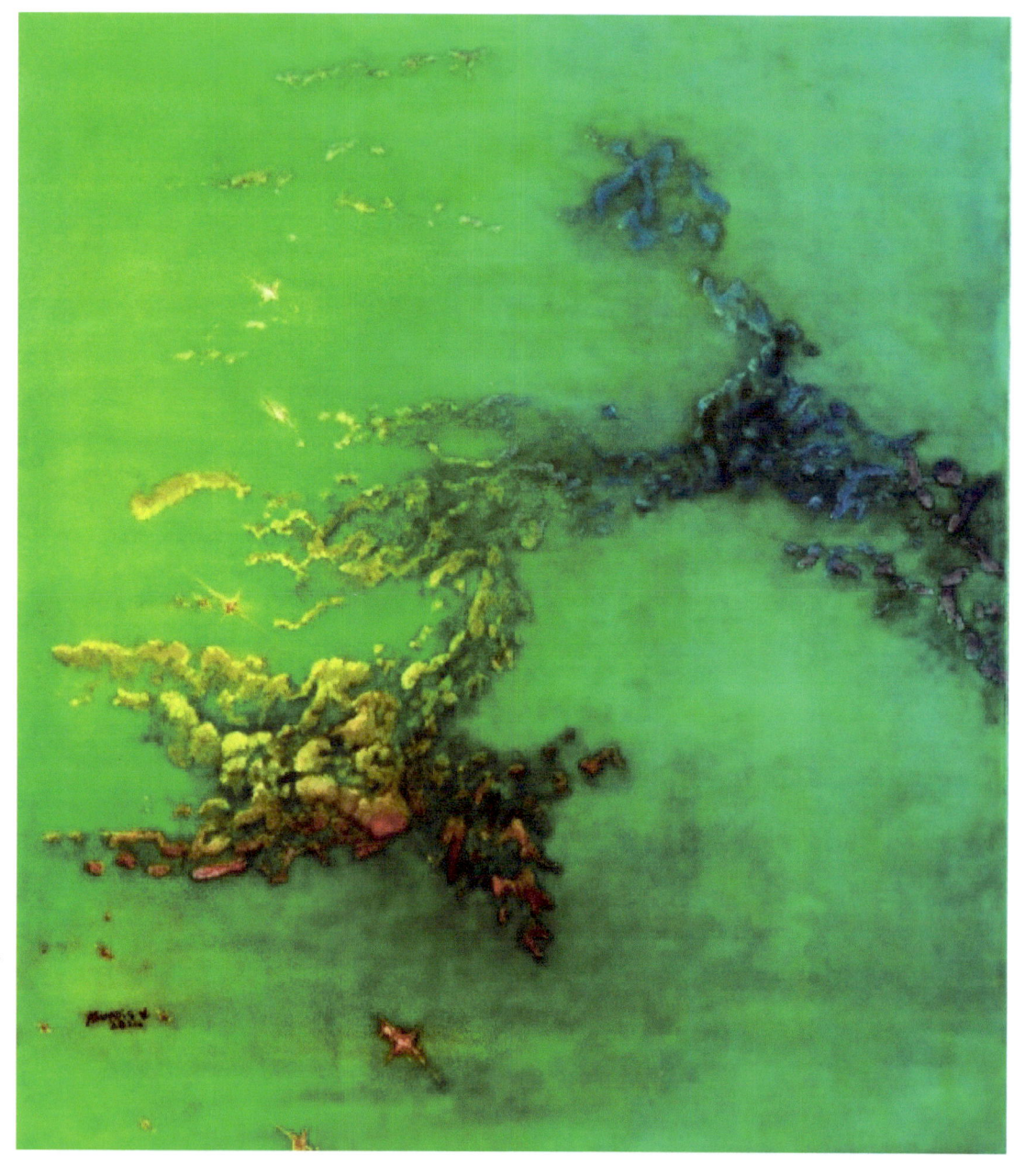

Oil on canvas, "The unverse, from darkness comes light"

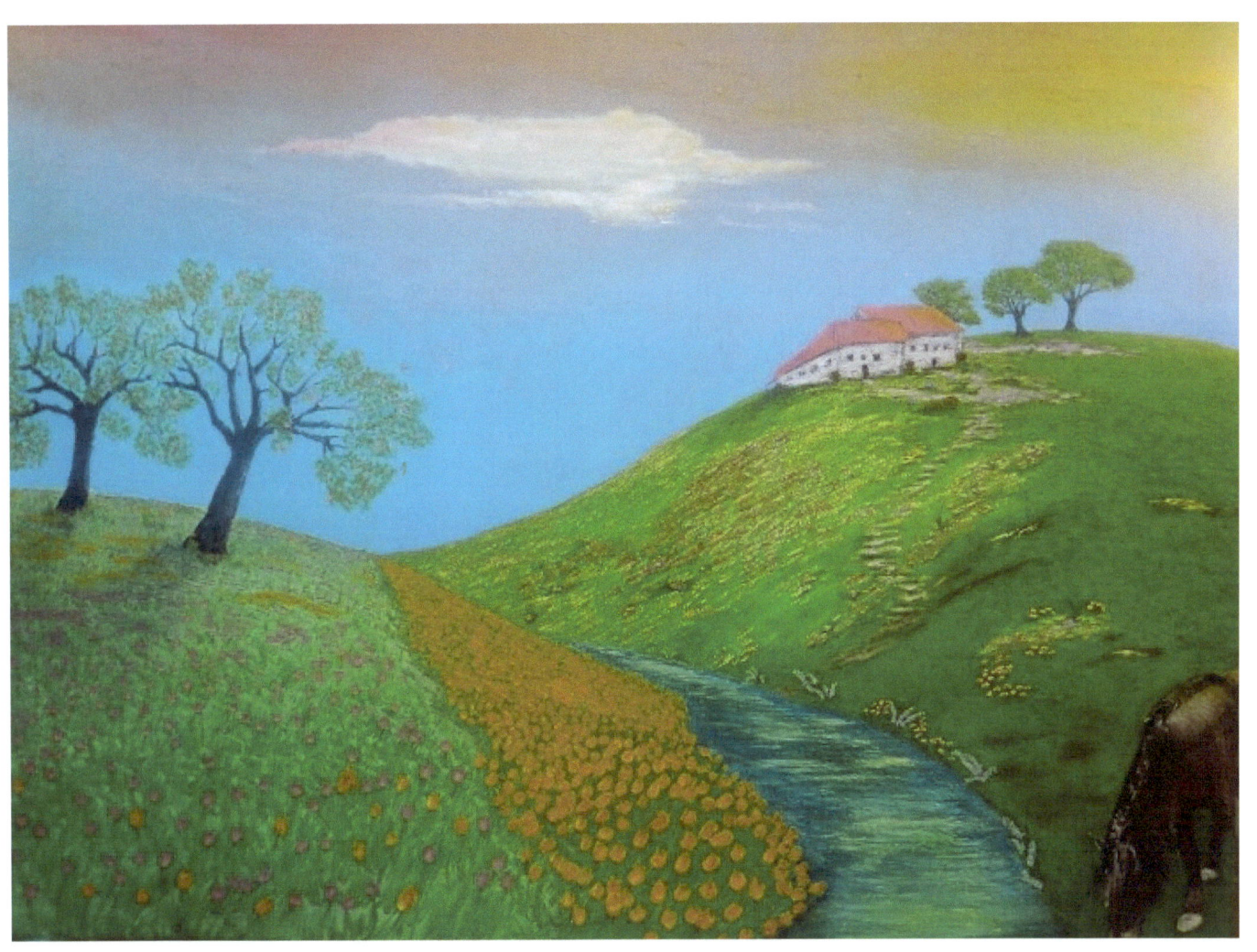

Oil on canvas, country scene

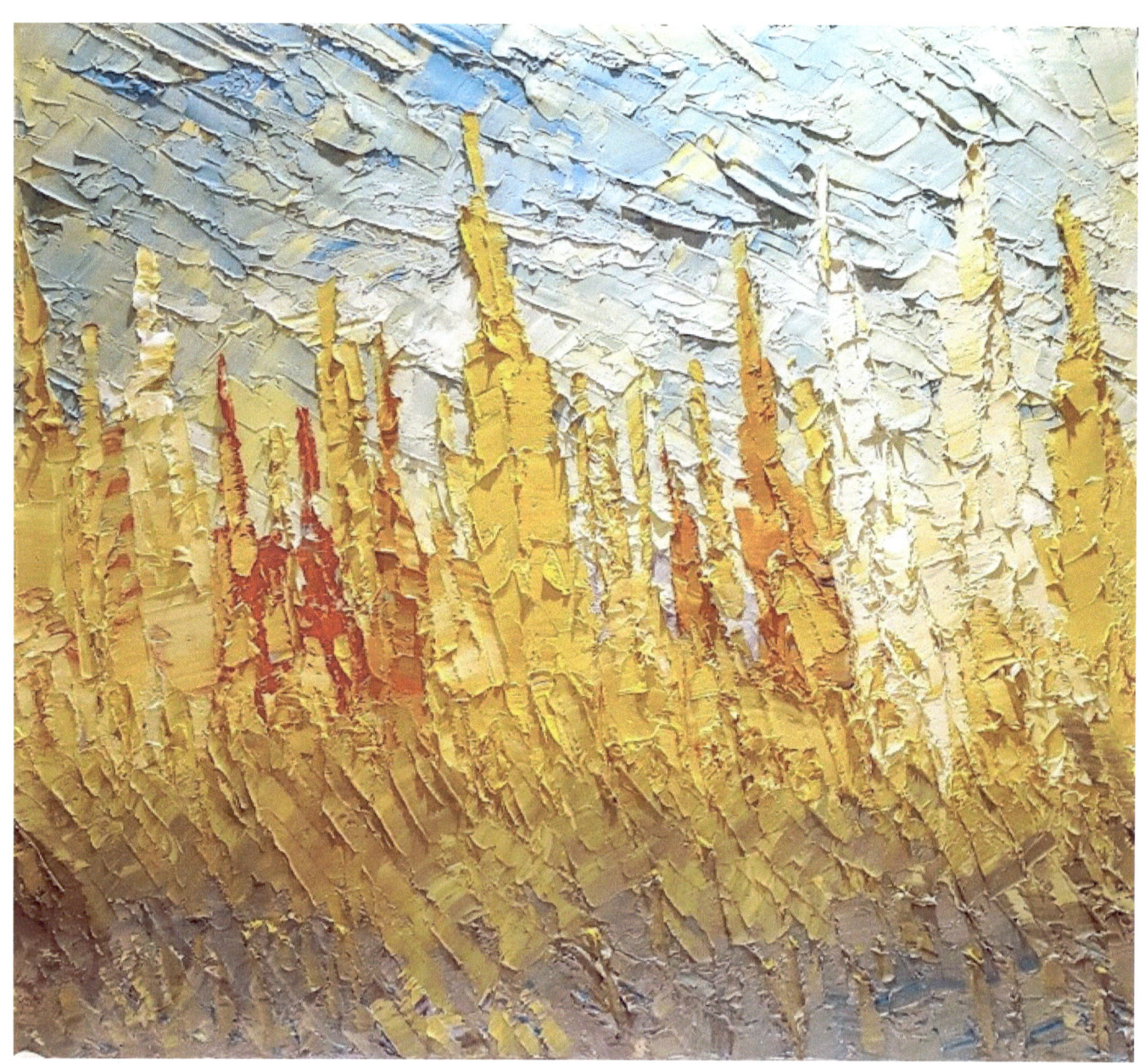

Oil on canvas, "city skyline"

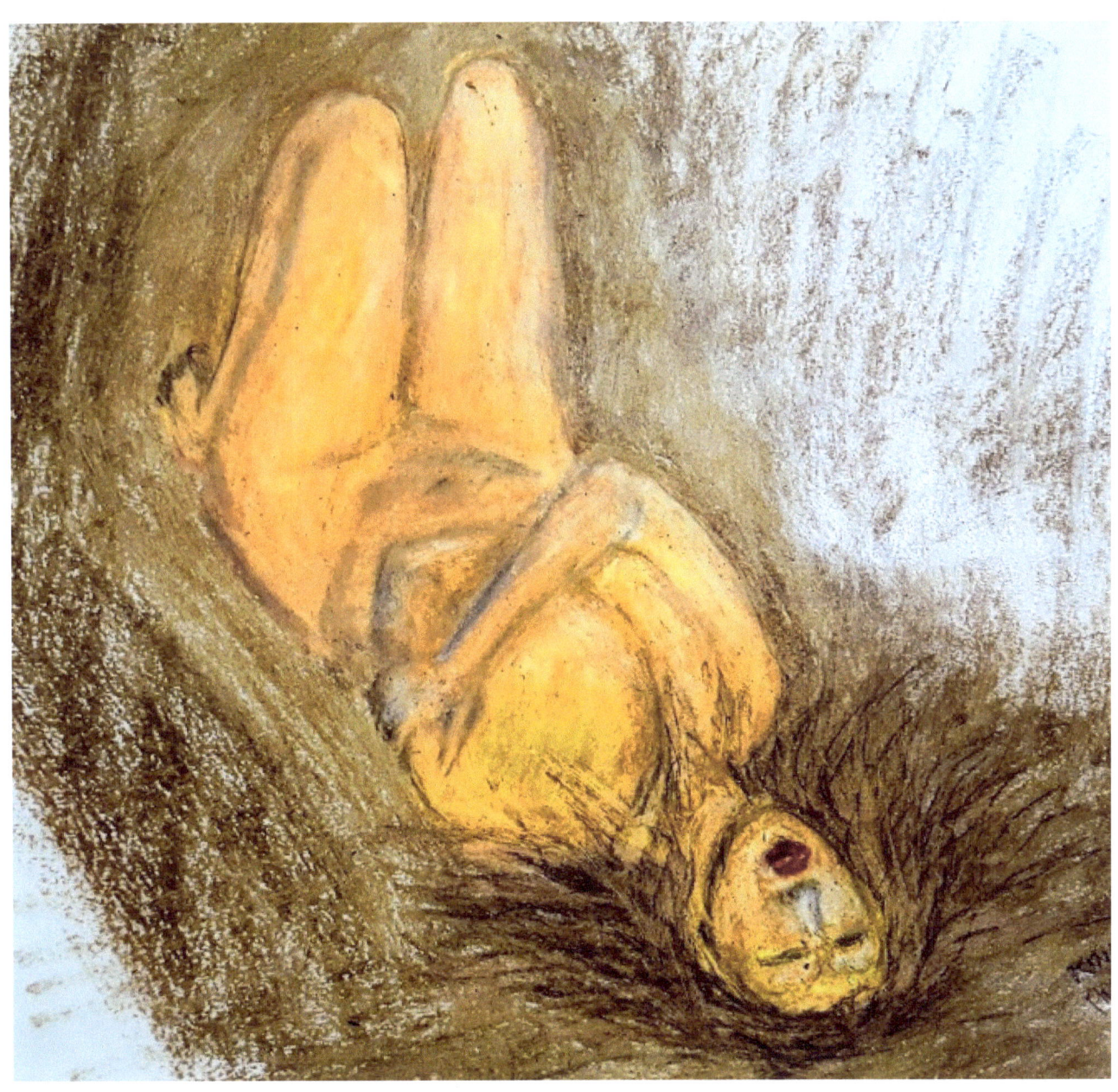

Color pencil sketch

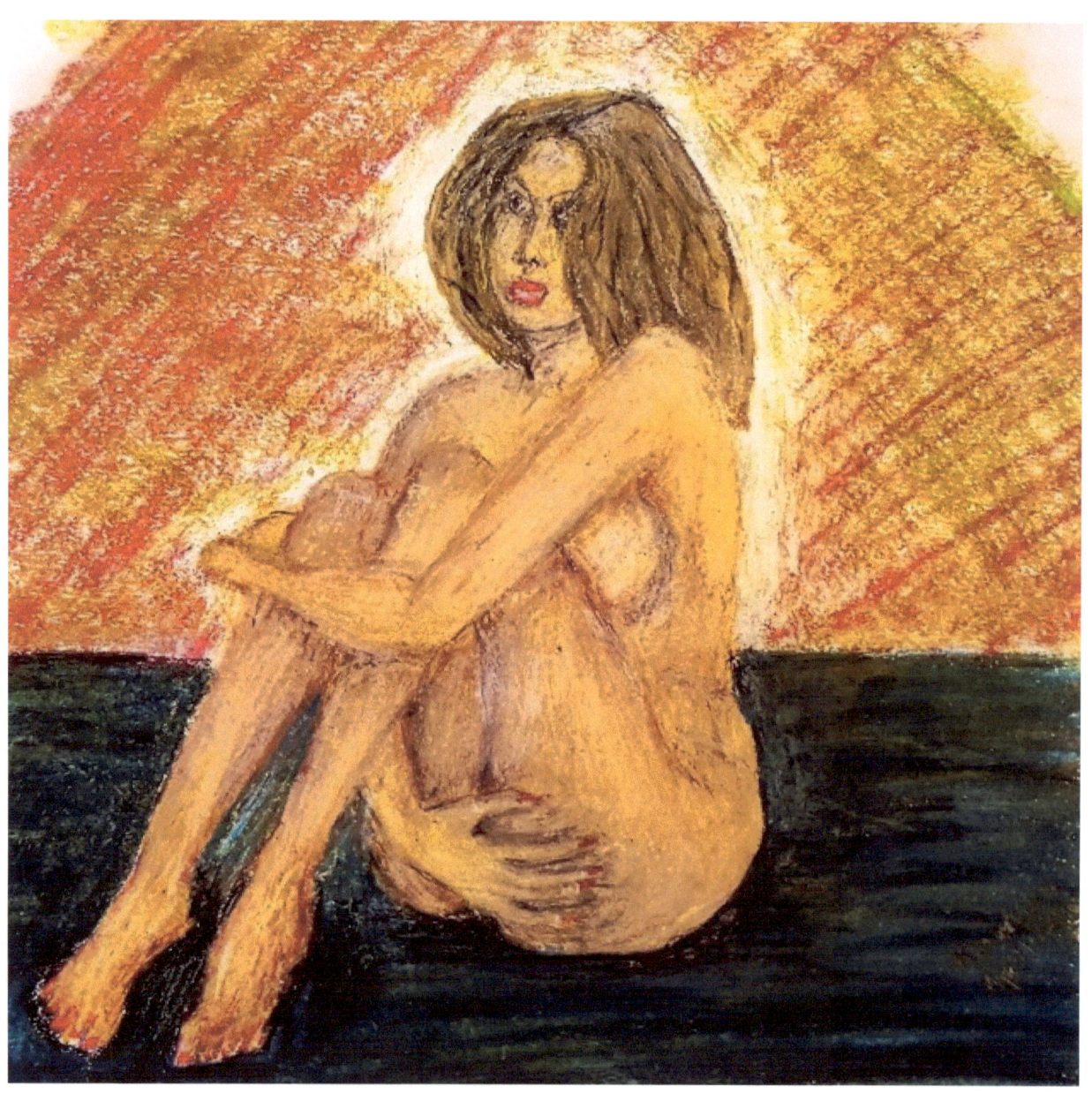

Color pencil sketch

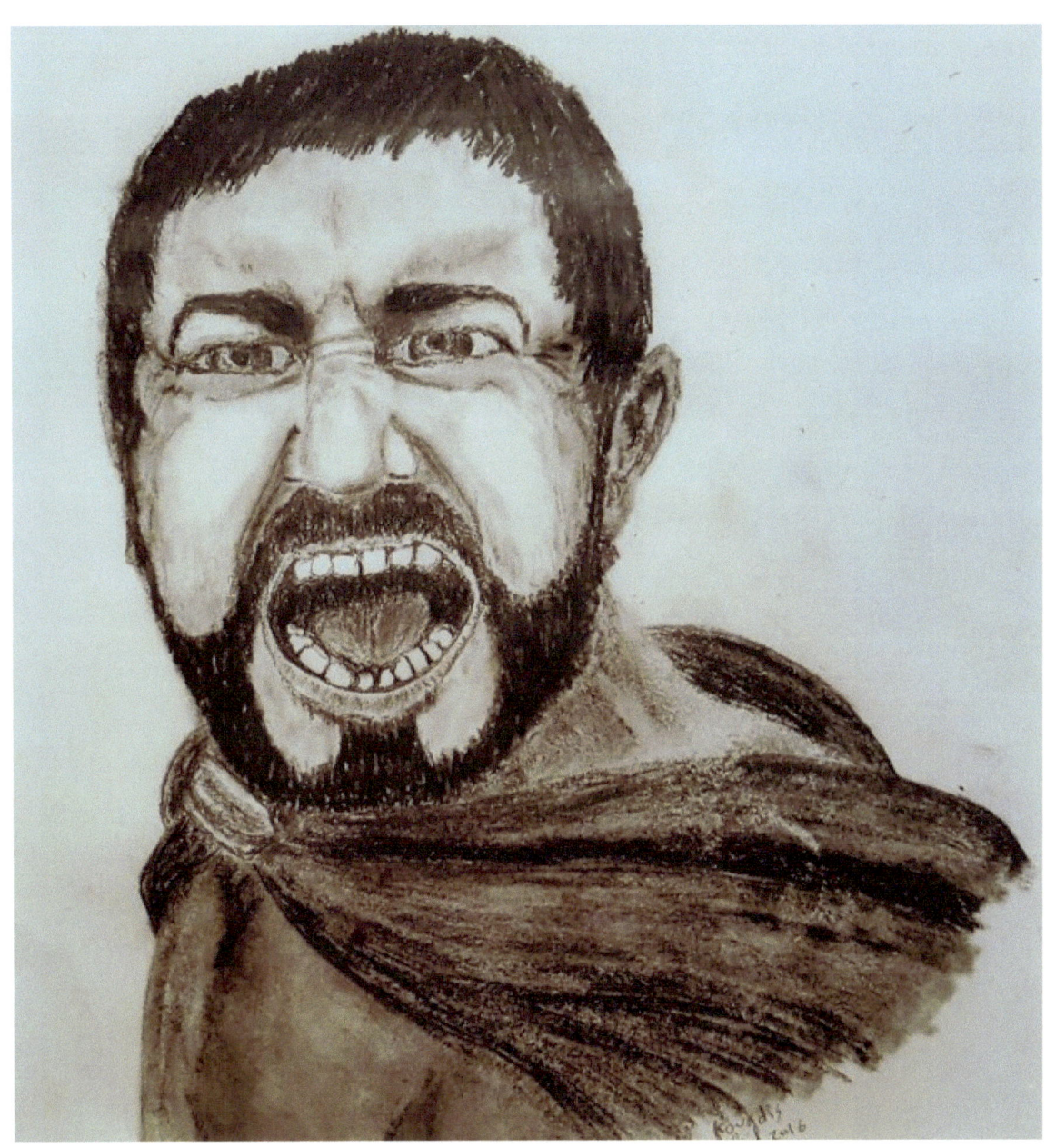

Pencil sketch

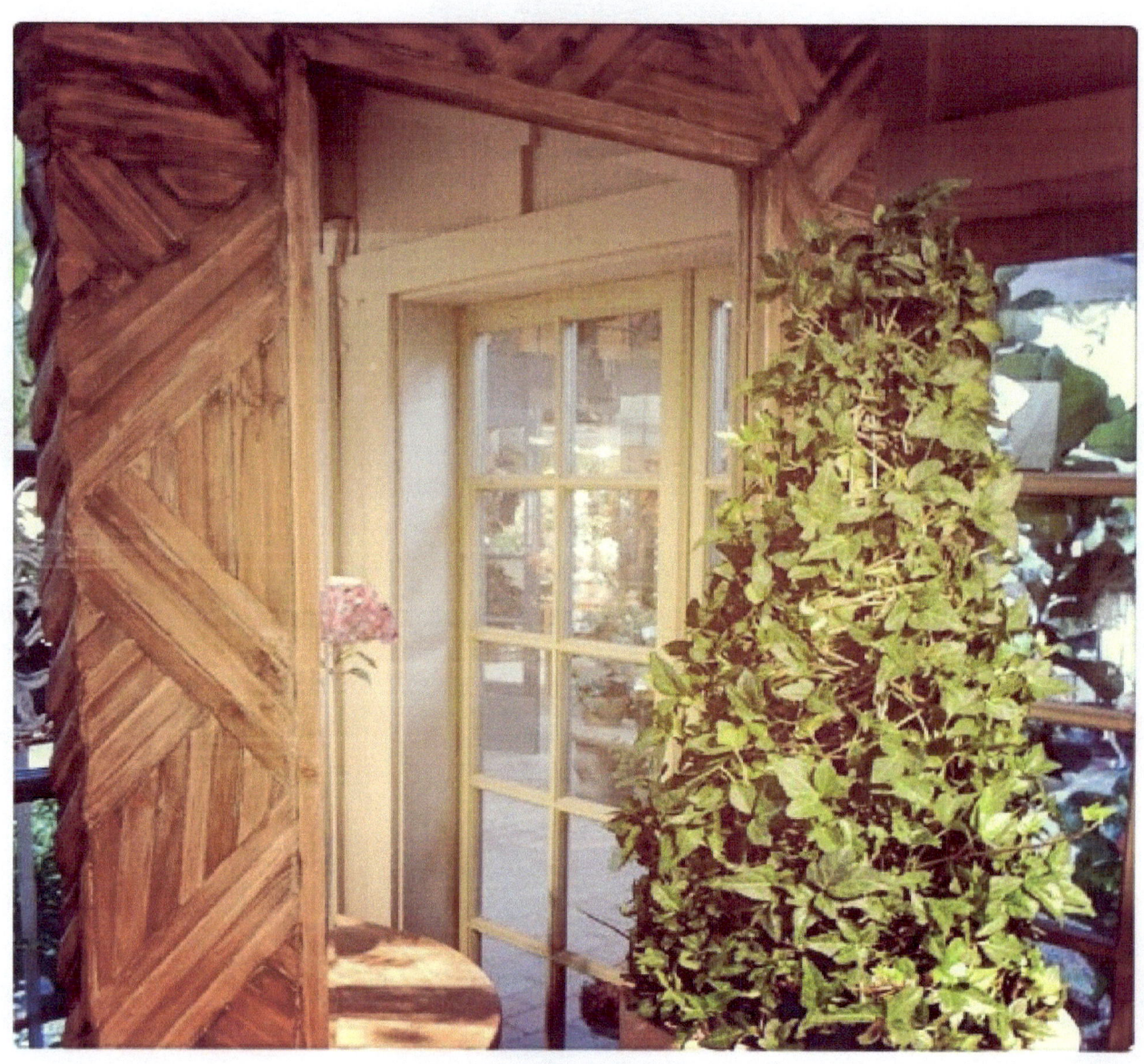

Random Photos of things, taken in LA

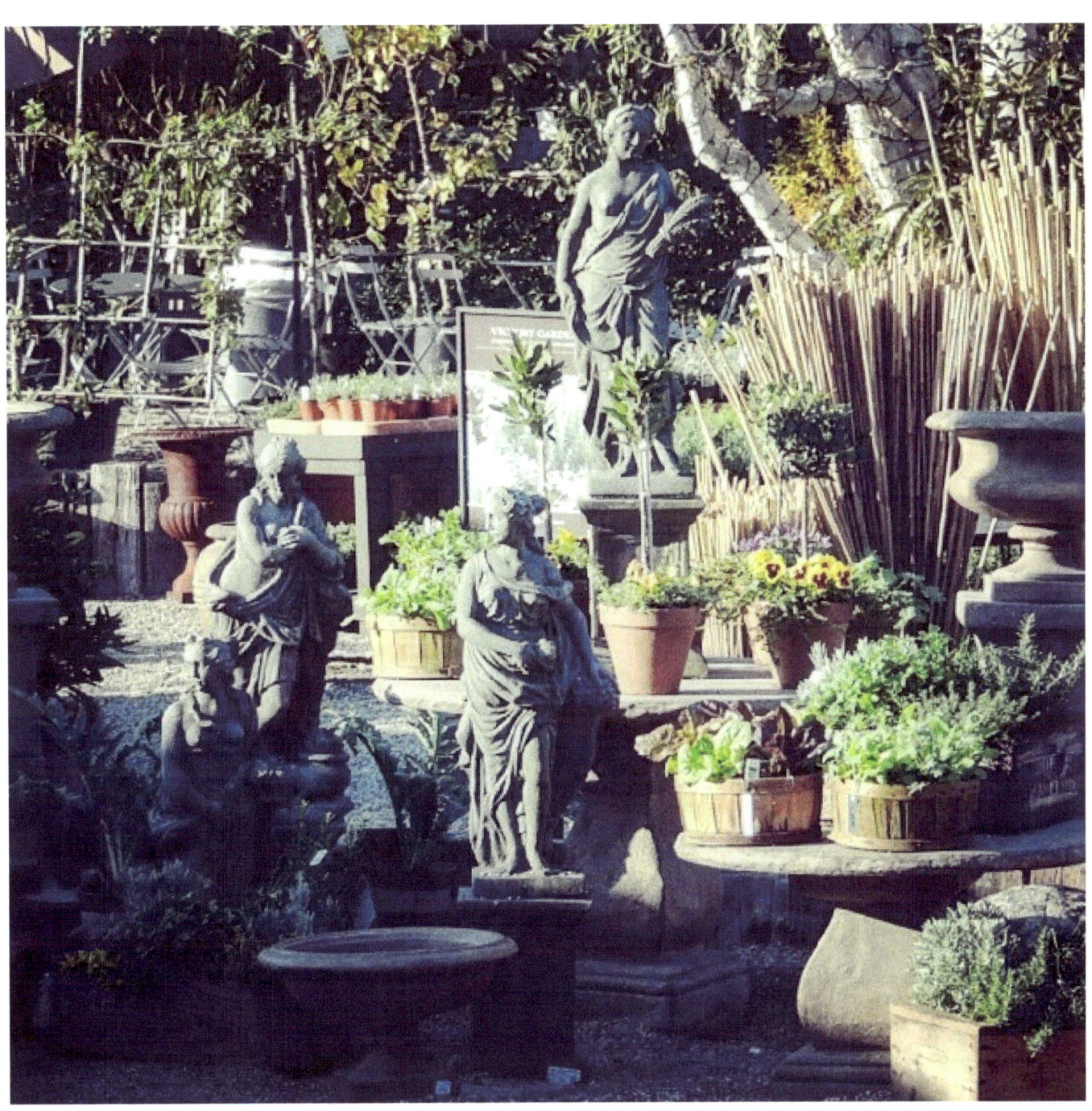

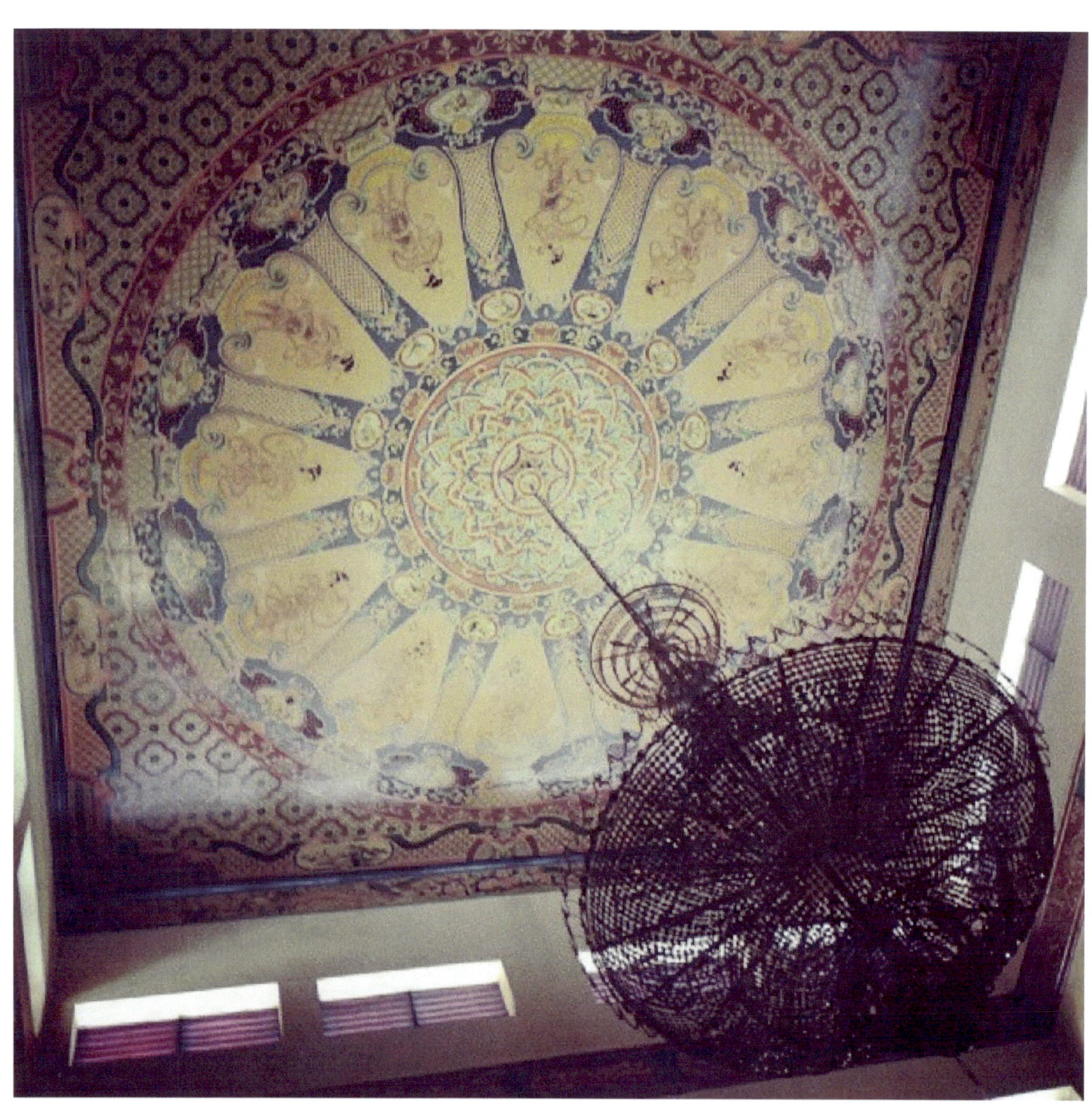

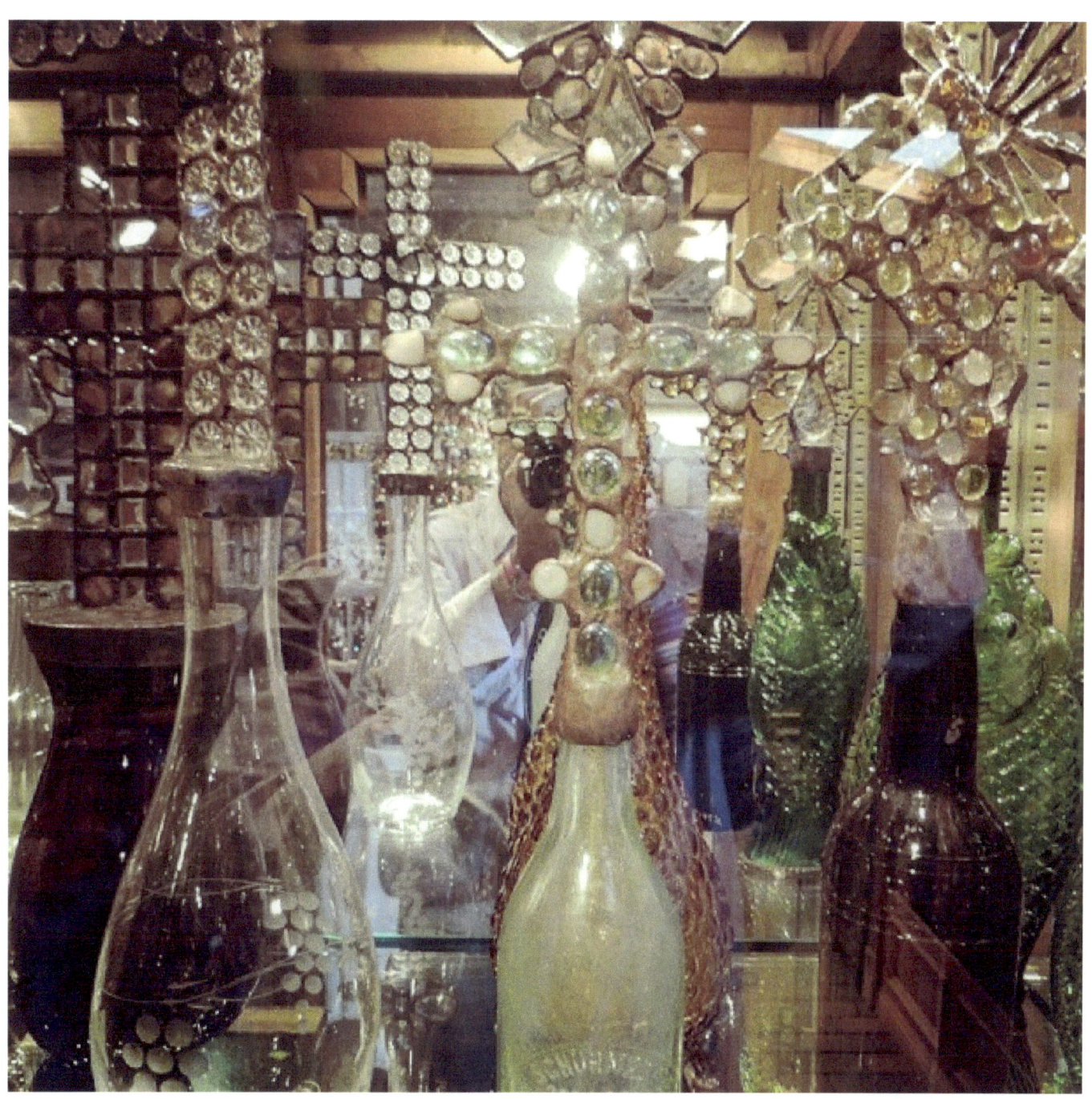

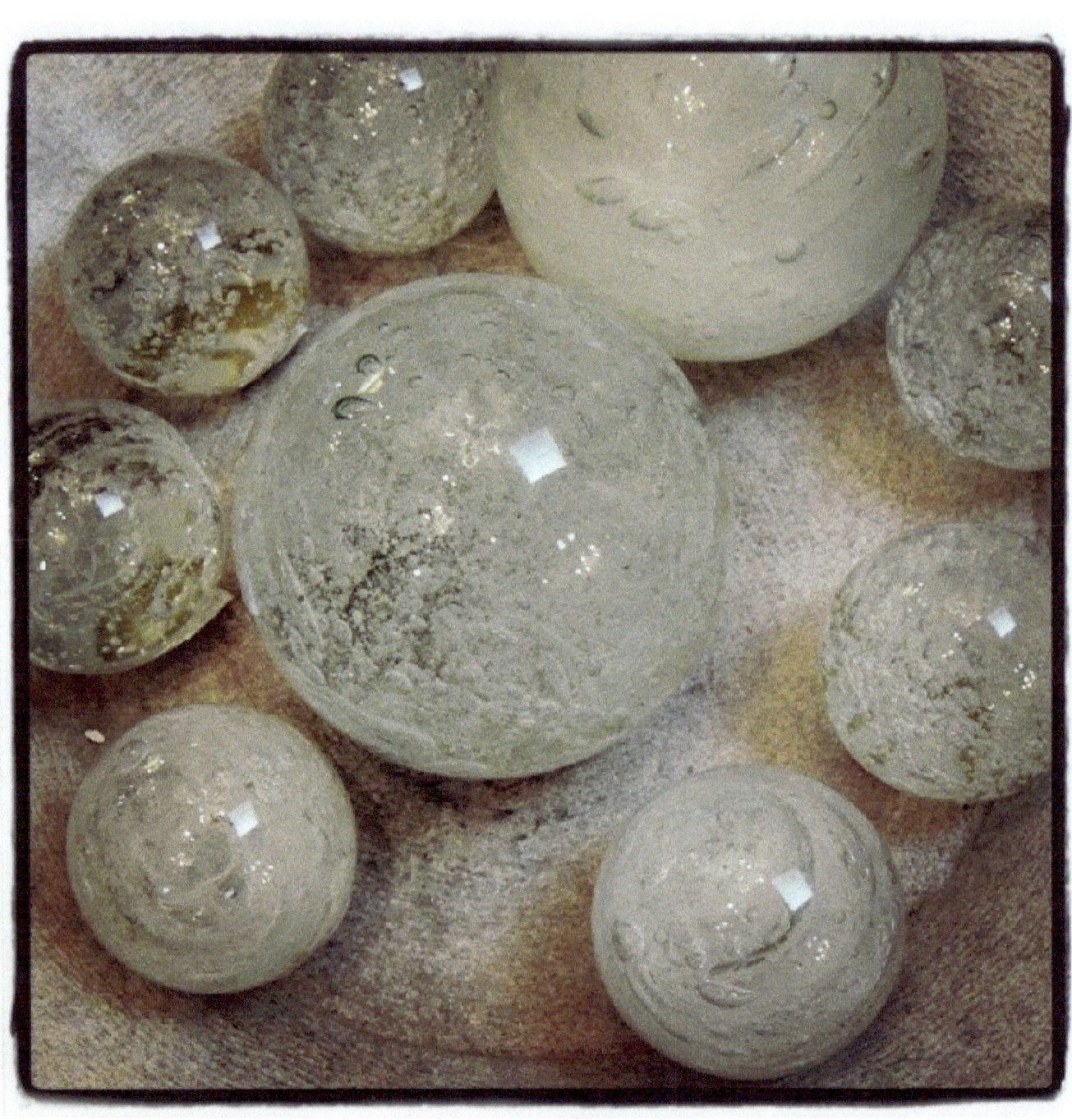

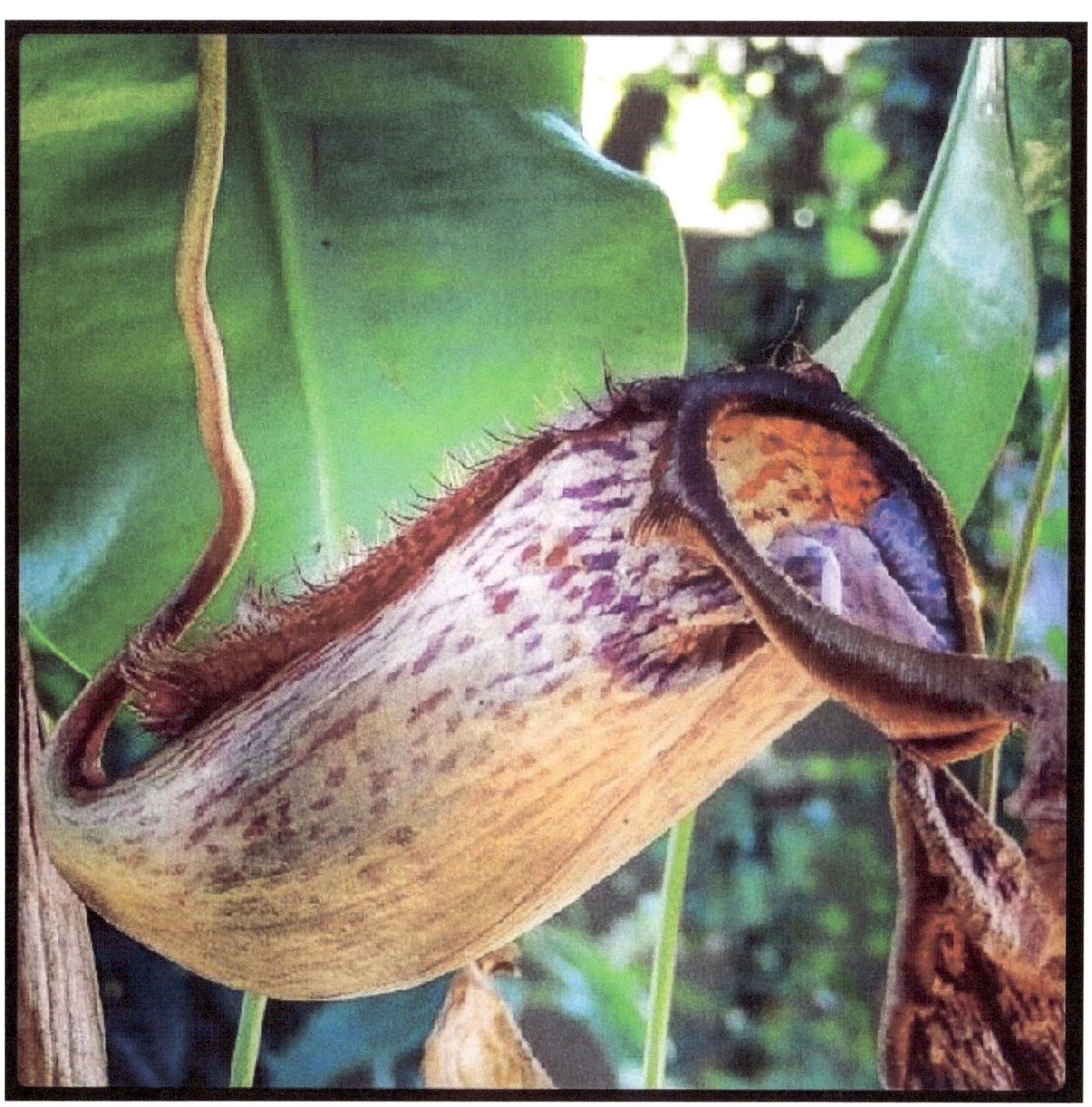

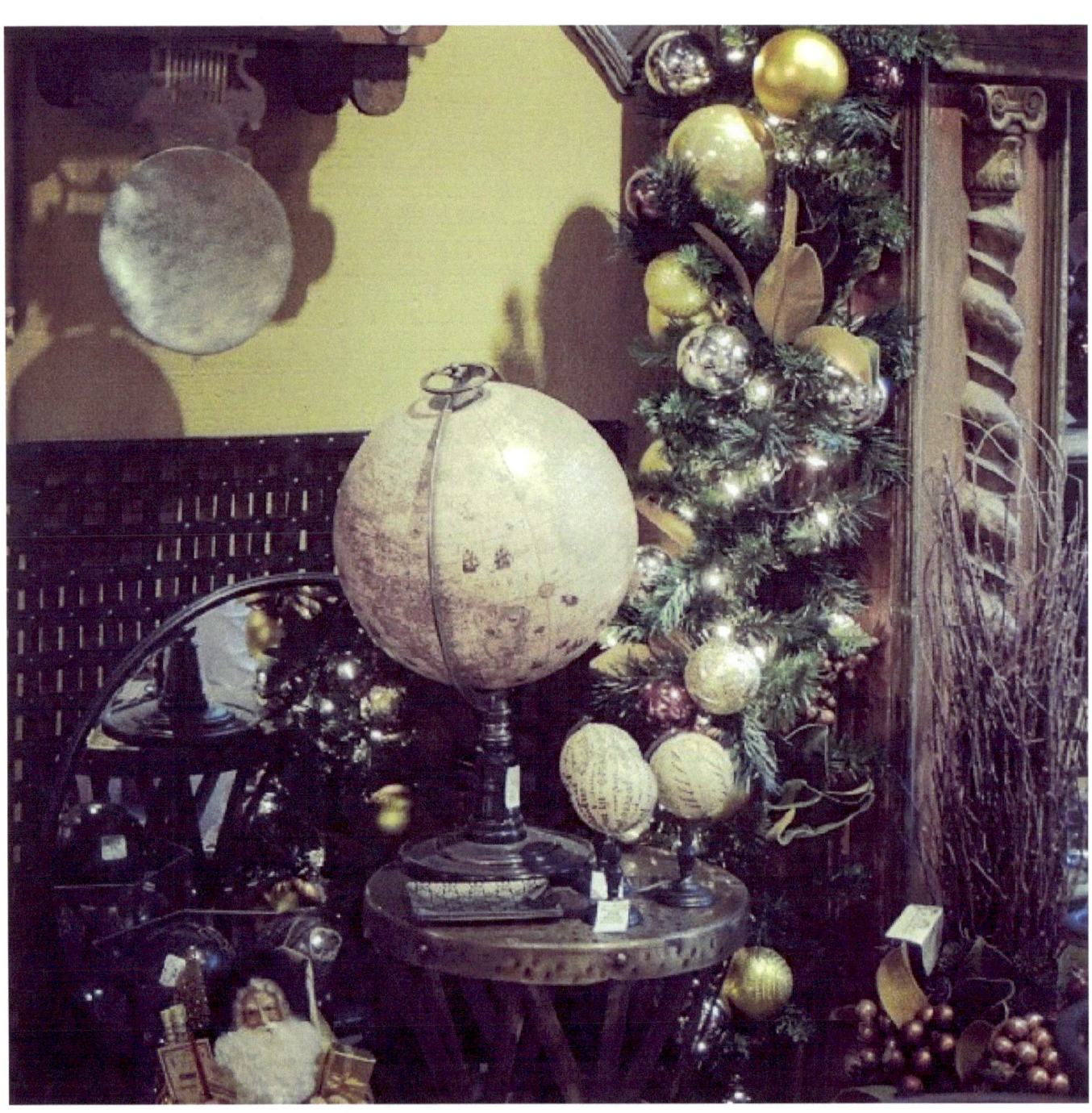

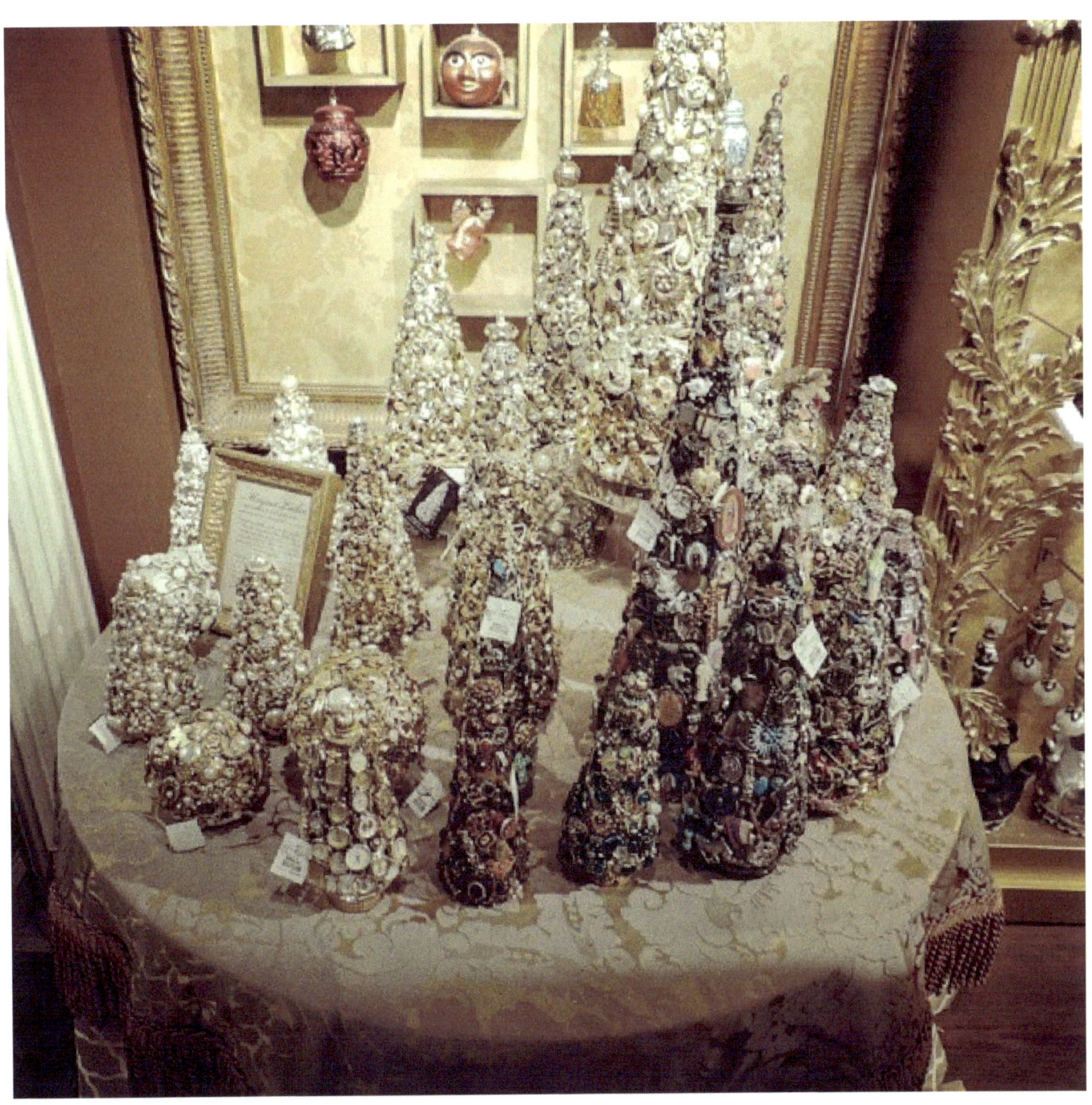

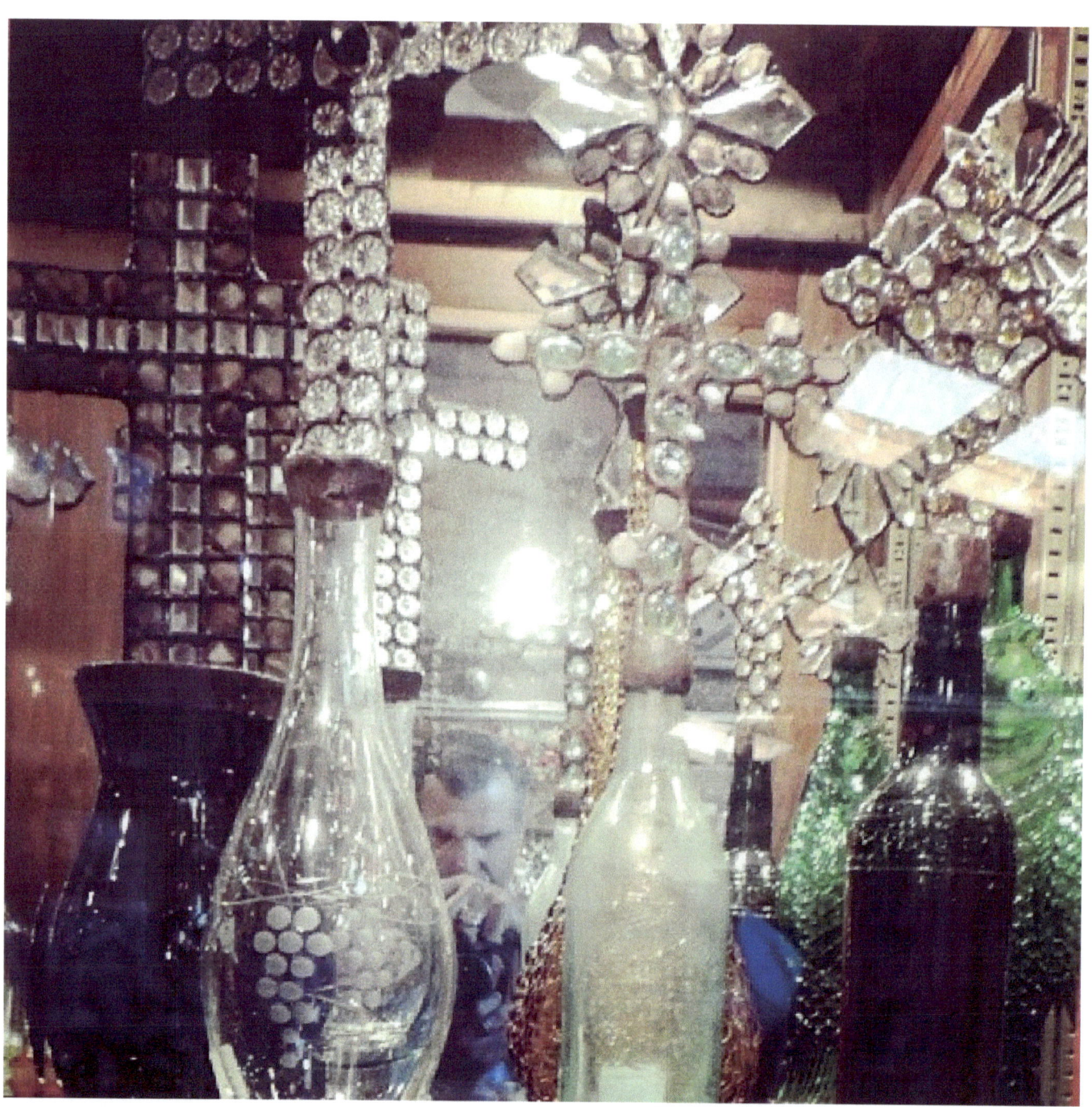

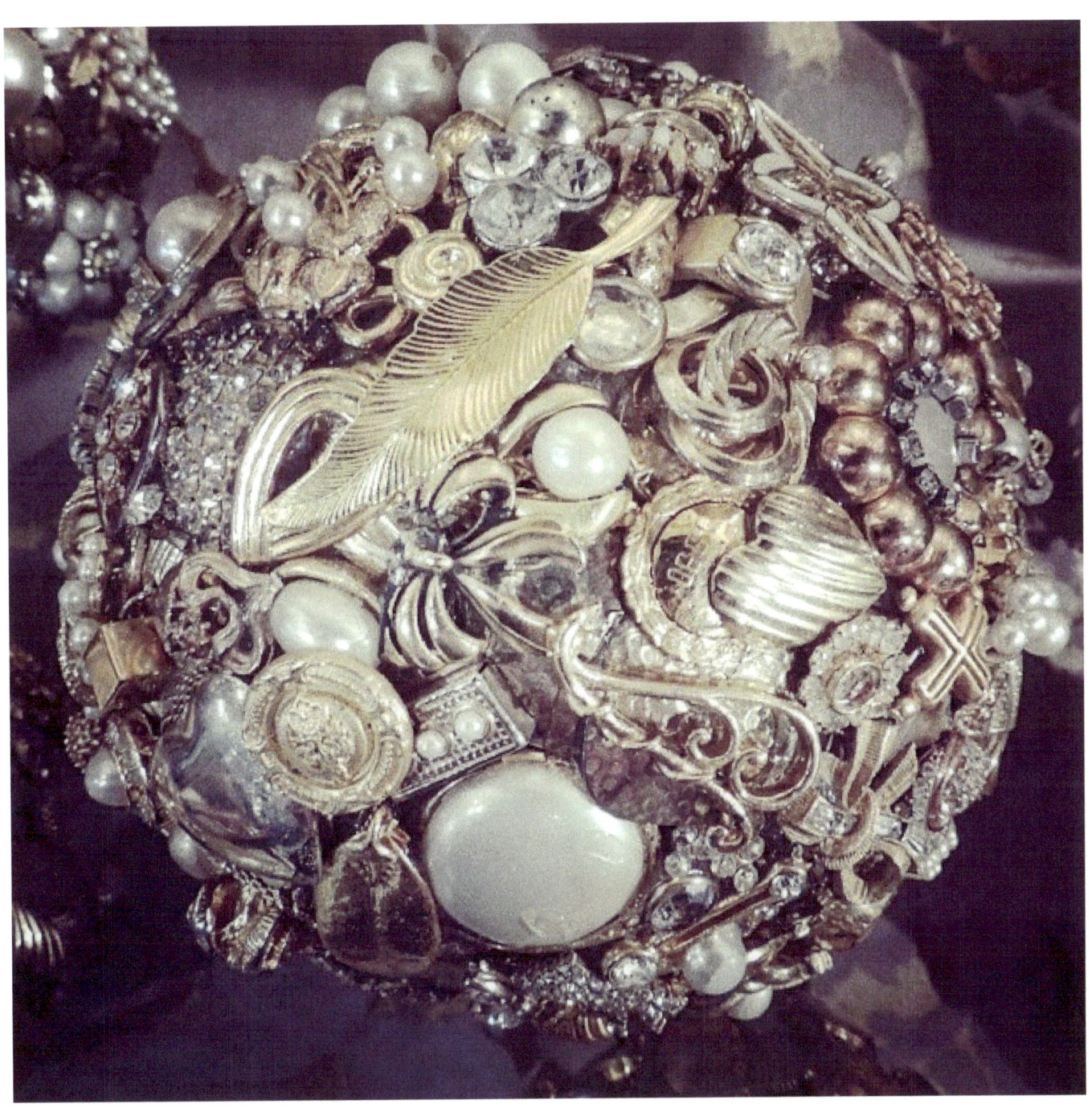

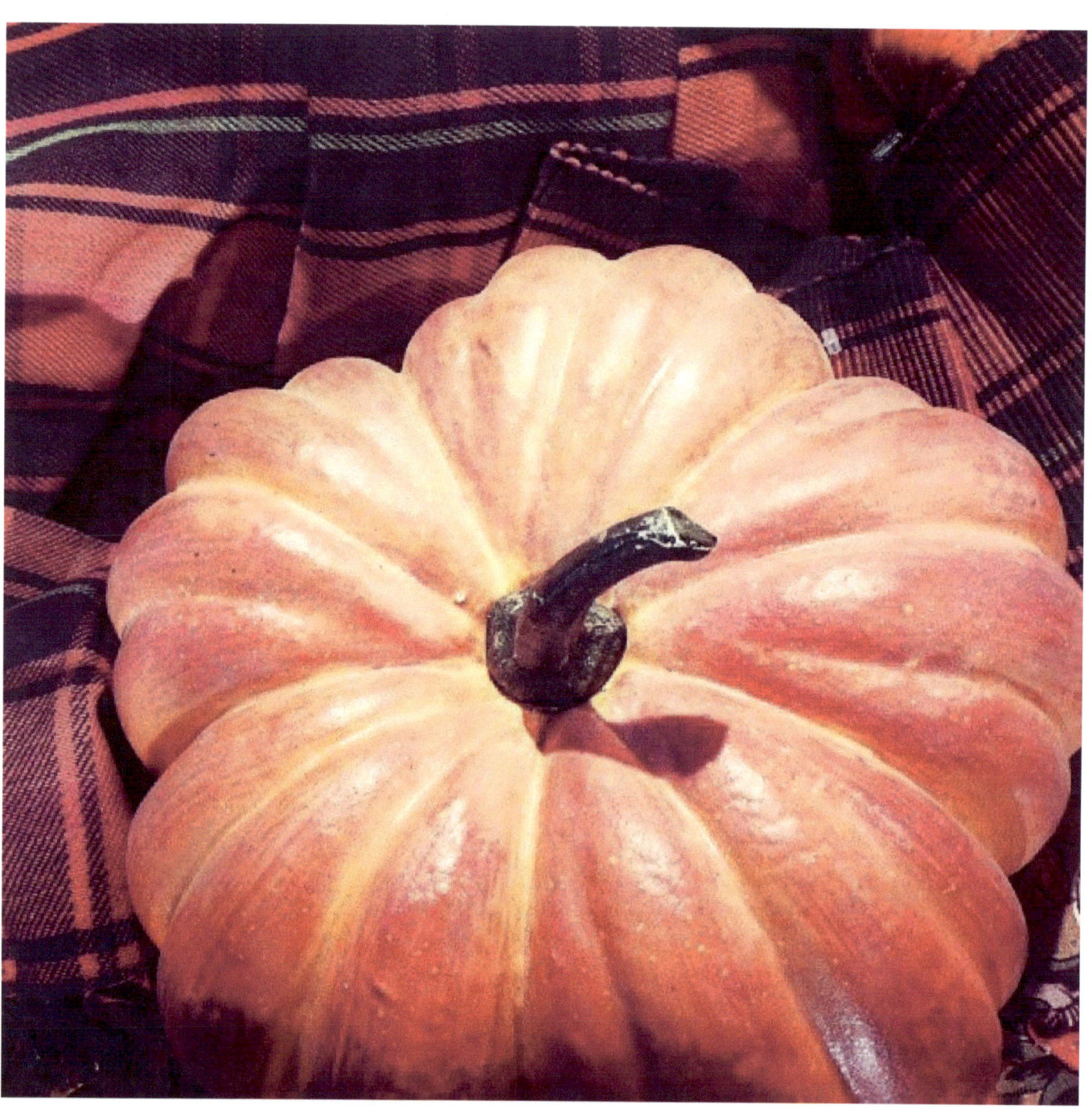

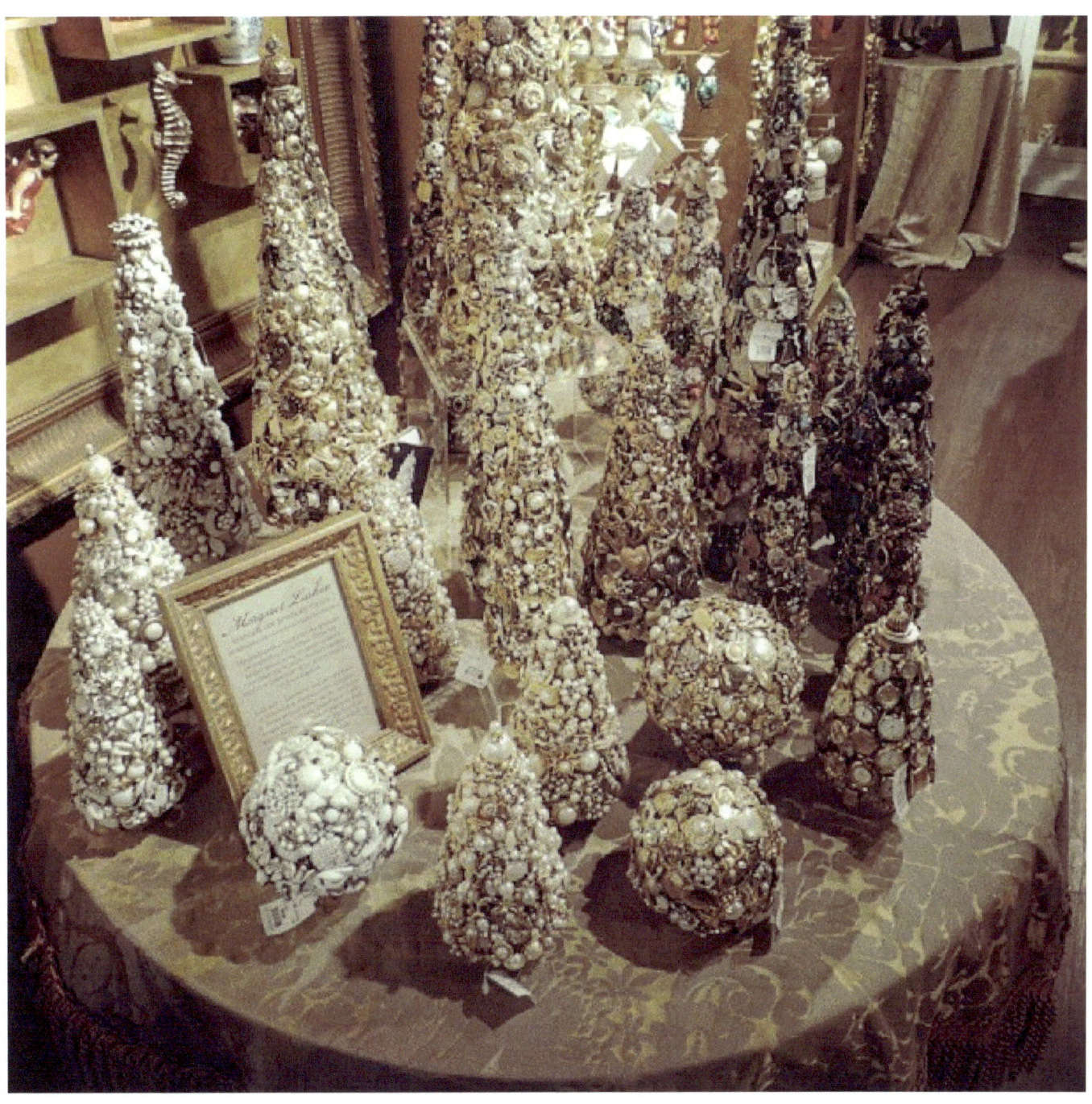

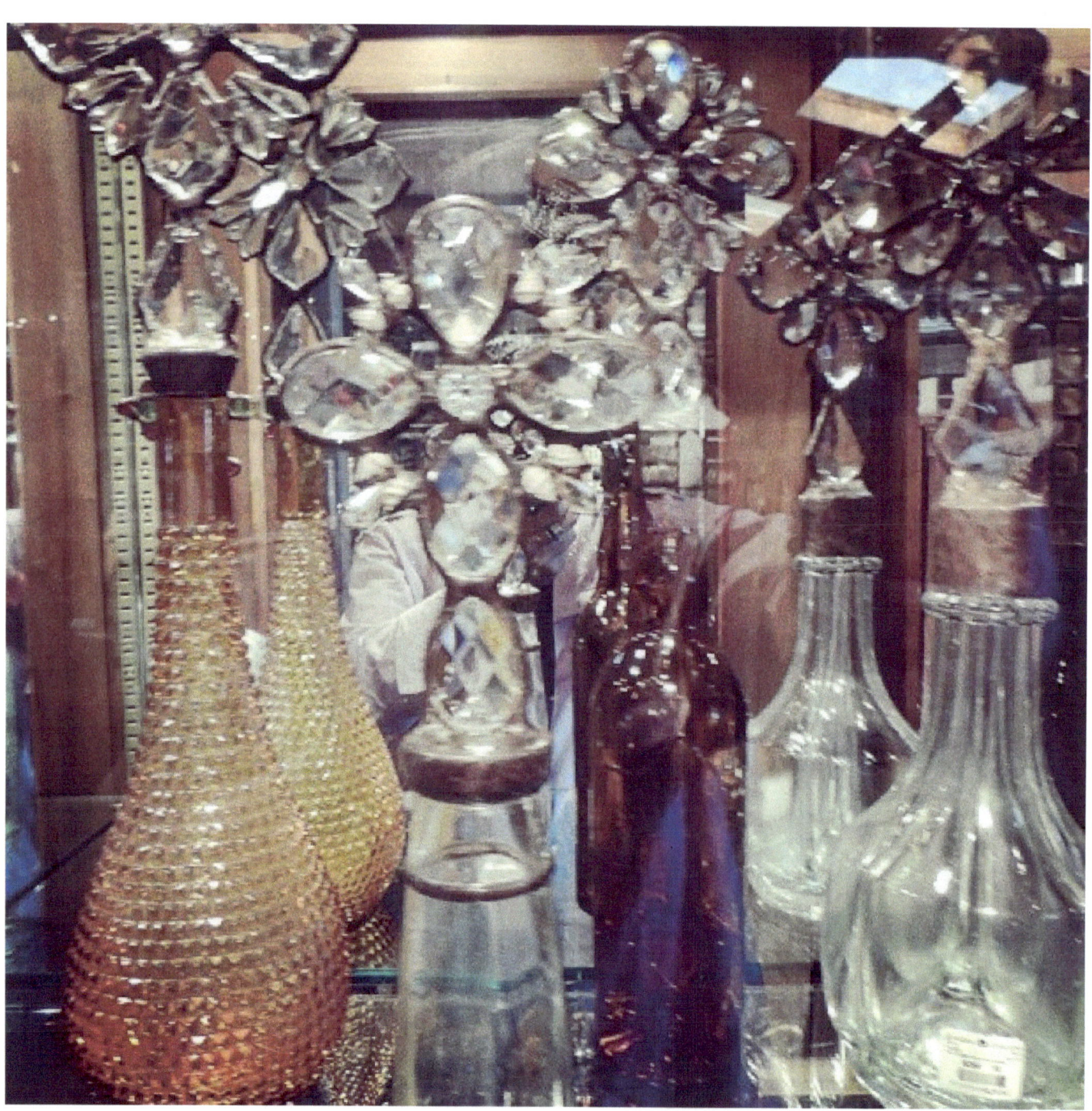

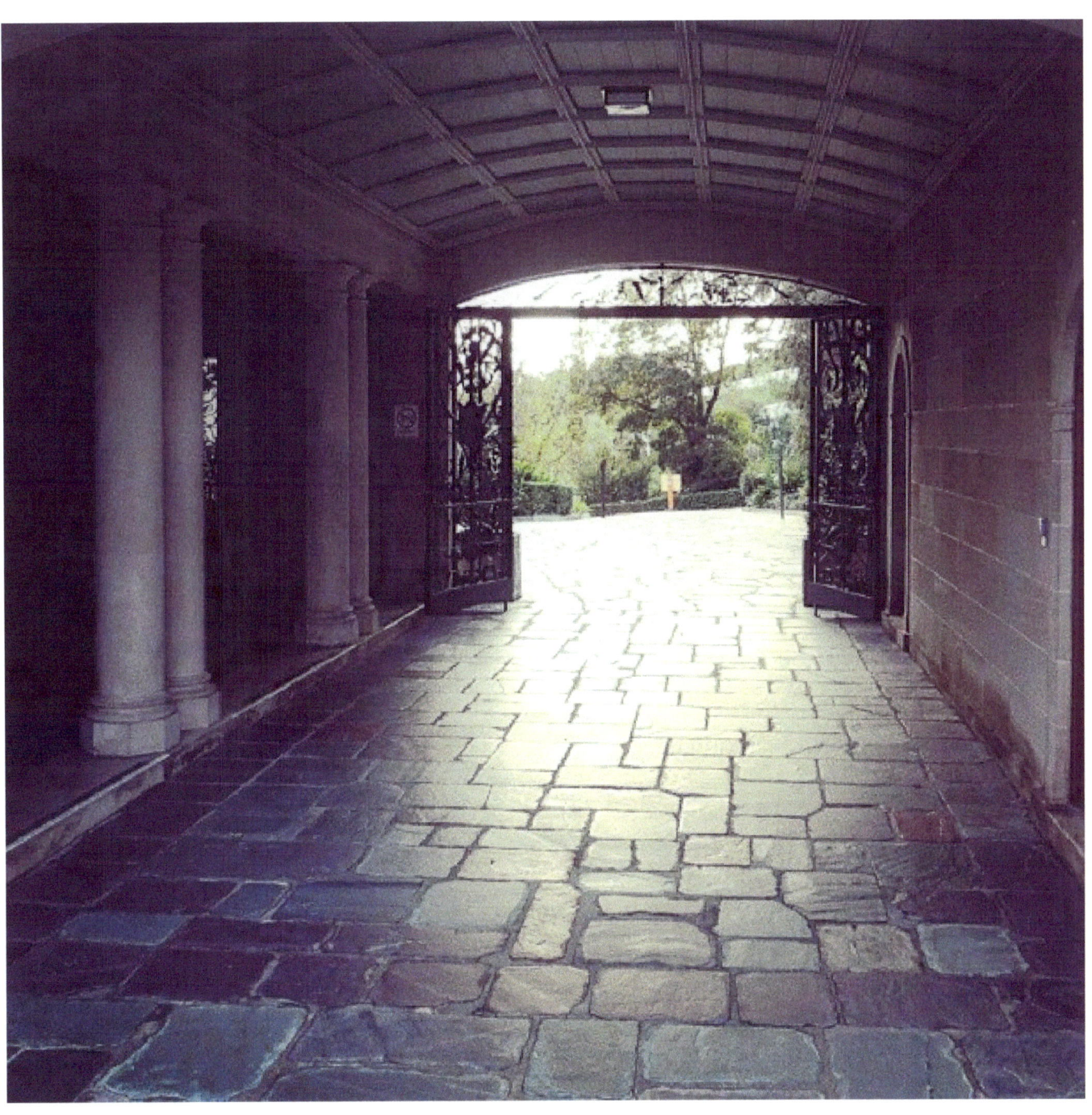

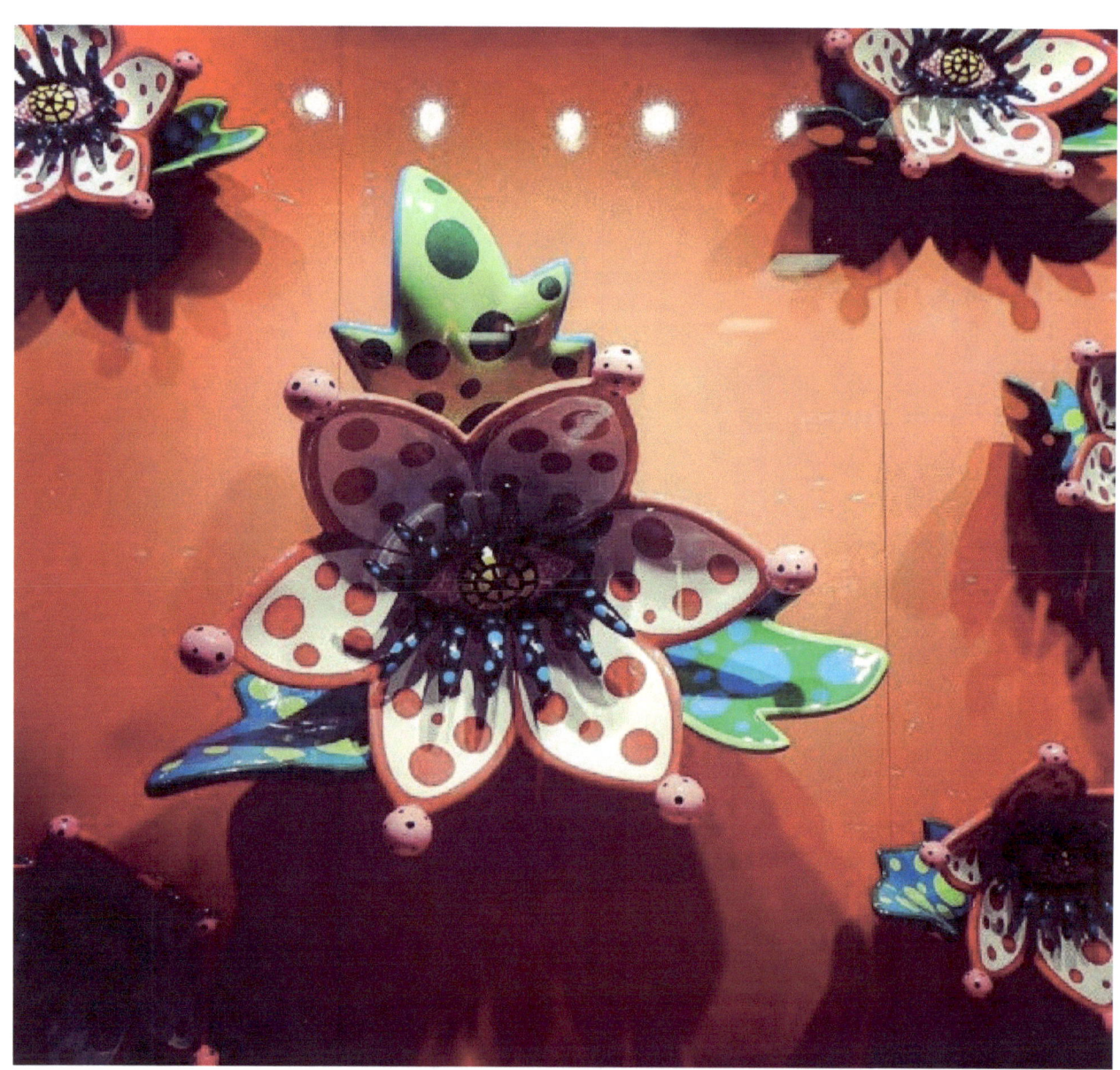

End of random photos of things taken in LA

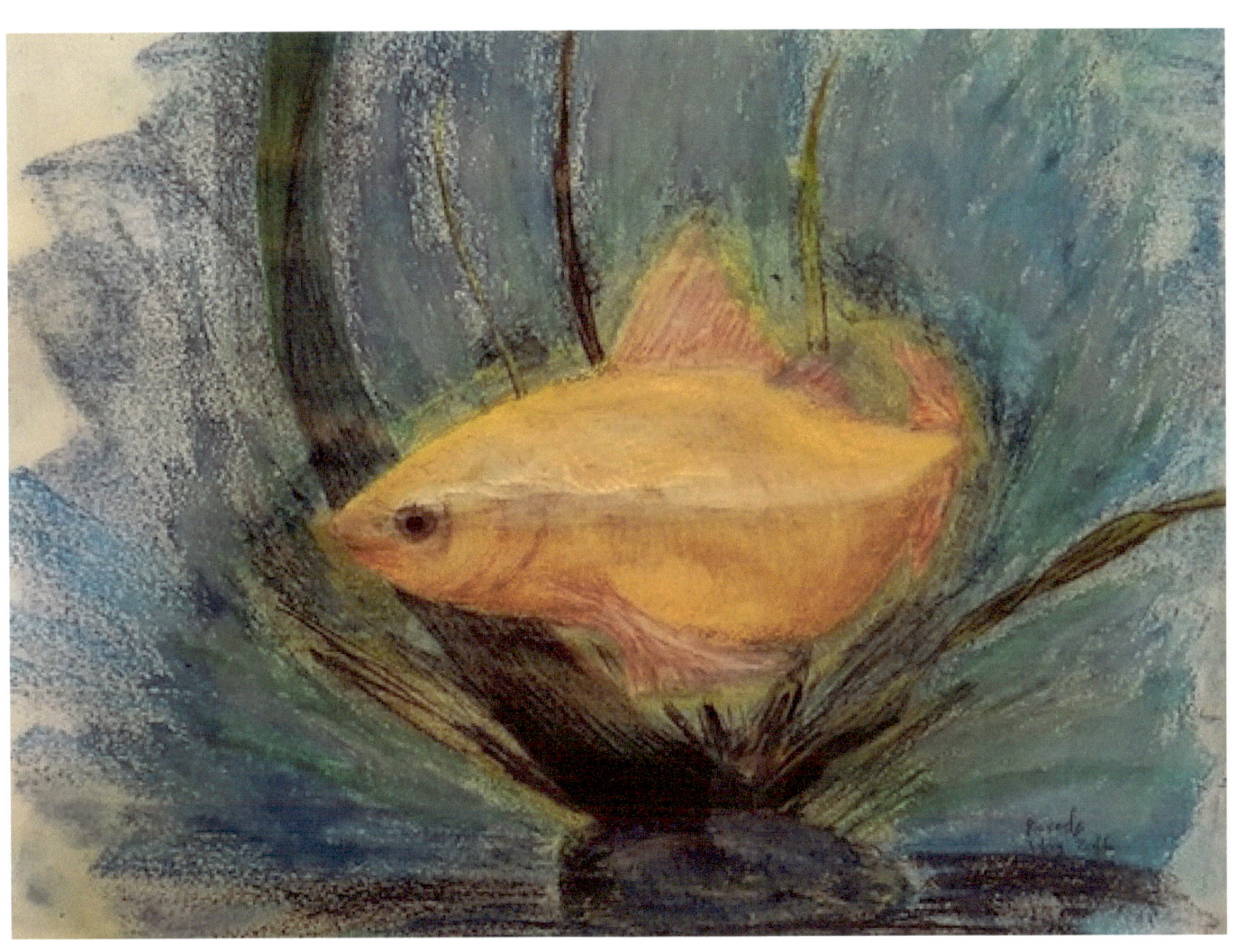

Color pencil sketch

Red flowers bloom upon the cheeks of fate, gliding through time eternal;
Like a young child's blush, with her eyes' curiosity unable to break the gaze.
This wise soul's deliverance, cautious and cruel and without rehearsal;
Honest in each step, blunt as she dances carelessly in the existence's maze.
With soft thunderous waves of joy heard by the ears of memories, and mine;
She sings the words of creation; she frowns at the dark and lends brightness to skies.
Note by note scored the spine of the universe to rhythms heartbeat, and sounds divine;
She spoke the symphonies of life to life, she tamed the rage of chaos, filled the minds eyes
With wondrous dreams sailing over stars and galaxies and oceans of light free.
She conquered awareness, blew a soft whisper into a wind, a destiny unknown;
Invisible ties pulling at every bend, every thought persuaded to return to see,
To stand still at the center of the clock, thorns tearing where roses have grown;
Searching horizons for a familiar sound, seeking home midst a bright blinding glare;
A Red flower's bloom, a scent, a call, a question; no answer. am I there?

Poem By Kovadis Najem

www.ingramcontent.com/pod-product-compliance
Lightning Source LLC
Chambersburg PA
CBHW041933240526

45473CB00034B/955